The Light Within You

Discover the power you've always had

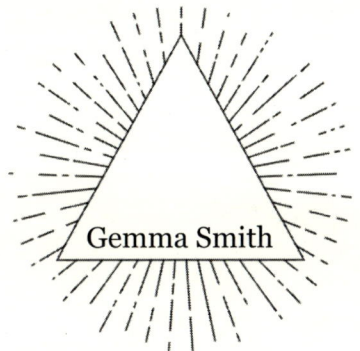

Gemma Smith

12561491

Copyright © Gemma Smith 2020

First published in Great Britain in 2020
Positive Side Ltd

Second Edition

London
www.thelightwithinyou.co.uk

Gemma Smith has asserted her right under the Copyright, Designs and Patents Act 1988 to be identified as the author of this work.

Every reasonable effort has been made to contact copyright holders of material reproduced in this book. If any have inadvertently been overlooked, the publishers would be glad to hear from them and make good in future editions any errors or omissions brought to their attention.

All rights reserved.
No part of this publication may be reproduced or transmitted or utilised in any form or by any means, electronic, mechanical, photocopying or otherwise, without the prior permission of the publisher.

Cover design by Sam Smith
Editing and design by Kaiesha Page
Formatted by Solaja Slobodan

A CIP catalogue record for this book is available from the British Library
Library of Congress Cataloguing-in-Publication

PB ISBN 978-1-8380477-8-8

eISBN 978-1-8380477-2-6

The Light Within You

Discover the power you've always had

Gemma Smith

UNITED KINGDOM – EUROPE - UNITED STATES -
CANADA – AUSTRALIA – NEW ZEALAND

Dedication

I wrote this book so that you are able to realise that you have a light inside of you that you can shine, truly embrace and share. A light that has the ability to transform your life if you use it wisely, and intentionally, and will benefit all of those who connect with your existence.

By reading this book you will be able *to discover the power you've always had*. You will realise that you deserve the best... You deserve to be, have and do all that your heart intends. You are important, and you *do* matter.

I dedicate this book to the miracle inside of you in the hope that the words and my voice touch and inspire you to do and become the very best version of yourself.

Love and Light

Gemma Smith

Table of Contents

Foreword 7

Why this book? 9

Enlightenment 15

Purpose 27

Bigger Than You 39

Rise Up 49

Lifelong Learner 61

Spread Your Wings 71

Super Strong 79

Sharing the Love 95

Reborn 109

Plant the Seed 123

The Power of Gratitude 135

Words 147

The Sunflower Shine 157

Life is Beautiful 169

Endorsements 181

About the Author 187

Gratitude 189

Note to the Reader 193

Foreword

We were born to be natural thinkers, curious and versatile. A skill innate, yet to many, unworldly in our normal day to day activities. Have you ever felt there is something missing in your life, although you seem to have it all? A career, a family, a routine... yet, there is something niggling deep within that you can't explain. It excites you and drives you insane, and it's all you can think about until you finally have found the answers you have been searching for.

Gemma Leigh Smith is the epitome of self-courage, determination, passion and hunger to go above and beyond her thirst to bring out the beauty in others, and her artistic thoughts create an impact like no other. One that shakes up the meaning of Pandora's box. Her appreciation for diversity and traditions, culture and travel, children and people have guided her to discover and fulfil that empty place, many never will in their lifetime. A triumph of reflection and achievement she will cherish, quietly satisfied of the footprints she will leave behind.

The Light Within You is a powerful self-help book that weighed heavily through her wisdom and the way she made me feel, absorbing and admiring the message through her words. I knew instantly, I wanted to know as much as I could about this mesmerizing individual and her passion to share her legacy. An exceptional and talented writer who has already captured the hearts of thousands.

Gemma, is a caring, accommodating and a passionate person. One whom I connected with

quite easily. Her tenacity and creative flare speak volumes as a humanitarian and an empowered woman that embraces humanity in all its glory. Gemma is a humble artist who is all about love, strength and the power to create awareness and educate mainstream society, reminding us all that beyond titles, materialism and an advanced digital age, there is a world out there that many of us will never truly grasp, the power of self-motivation, positive vibes and energy that teaches us how to cushion our reaction at all that life challenges us.

Gemma's life experience is her distinct signature in the world of hope. Her ability to bring out the colour, beauty and individual strengths in each person has won Gemma international recognition as a journalist, writer and a humanitarian around the world. A whirlwind of solace and incredible talent, the epitome of ingenuity at its best. The Light Within You is the light within all of us!

Jasmina Siderovski
International Gold Winning Author – Philosophy
CEO and Editor-in -Chief eYs Magazine

Why this book?
Feel and be inspired, not tired

We are all ordinary people, though ordinary people can sometimes do extraordinary things by shining a light in a dark room.

Have you ever wanted to do something so bad that it never actually happens? You think about it tirelessly, only to find your burning desire to do it increases over time. You know that you should be doing something, but something keeps stopping you. See, I once heard that we are most afraid of what we can achieve and that fear alone can prohibit our success. But everybody has the ability to become the best version of themselves. Why? You and I have a light inside of us... a light that can not only change your life but also has the power to impact others, significantly. We have the right to operate on our highest potential and whatever it is we want to do in this world, we can use our light to truly ignite the flames.

Inside this book, I am hoping that you will discover that you have always had the power within you to become the person you are meant to be.

While writing this book, I had the idea to create my own quotations for each of the chapters. I hoped that this would help to enhance the meanings conveyed throughout this book. While the contents of this book will help you to rediscover your light and live a life that is more filled with love and joy, these quotes will hopefully reaffirm everything that you learn. Grab a notebook or some sticky notes and write theses quotes down as you go along.

Carry them with you, place them in places where you will constantly see them or use them when you need them most. Let them light you up as you continue through your day and remind you of the wonderful lessons that you are learning with me.

Sometimes you may feel stuck in the darkness but remember that you are not alone. I have been that person stuck in the darkness for a very long time... I have put off something that truly mattered to me purely because I felt afraid of being judged. I knew from a very young age that I wanted to write and always dreamed of writing my own book. Why did I feel that way? I knew that I enjoyed expressing myself through words and it made me feel happy. When something makes you feel happy, that's a sign you're on the right track. You are in alignment with yourself... you are on the right road of discovering who you really are, and you can then take steps to fulfilling your truest potential. That is what I'm hoping you can gain from reading this book.

Don't worry about failure, failure is natural... after all, to fail just means it's your First Attempt In Learning (FAIL). You and I are both learning every single day whether you realise it or not. There is true magic in realising that, embracing that and accepting that as a truth, because it reassures you that you are always growing. As human beings, we are learning and developing continuously, even when we think that we're not. All around us we are surrounded by information. In all areas of life, we are absorbing different messages from people, from inanimate objects, events and from nature. We are digesting so much information that some may call it 'information overload', because we can often feel

very 'overloaded' internally. This makes it even more important and essential that we are *awake* and that we give ourselves the love, nurturing and belief that we deserve.

It's not about creating a perfect moment, it's about being in the moment and making it perfect for *you*. Even if you don't know your life art right now or you can't have your life art just yet, you need to set yourself up with the right qualities to lead you on to greatness. In all that you do, do it with all of you, put your values and your attitude that you would apply to your life art towards a job that you may not be happy with, so that you become a master of self with self-control. <u>You need to create an infinite love inside of you for all that you do and in all that you are because you know that your ultimate right and worthiness is to be happy.</u> You need to create that connection to your life art within your job/everyday life... so for example, if you are working in an industry that may involve numbers but your life art is to become a musician, you could see and relate to numbers as music notes in order to spark the flame inside of you and bring out the best side of you that you have to give to the world. When you do finally reach your life art you will be ready for it with all that you need to truly represent someone empowering and rightful for that position. You need to take control over your life. Take back the power. The power that you've always had...

Light is a beautiful and simple word, but it can mean so much and make the world of difference. When you think of what light can do, it can brighten up a room and offer a sense of direction. Light enables us to navigate our way around and without it, we rely on our other senses more. When we think of human light, we are referring to our internal, warm energy. An energy that lives inside all of us. We each radiate our own energy and have our own internal light that we have the power to share with other people. We have an empowering ability to transform lives with this light, to manoeuvre people out of the darkness, to rid the rain and invite the sunshine.

Everything you have been through has led you to this moment. I can proudly say that I have been left with no choice but to share this knowledge with you. As I like to say, *sharing is caring*... I had a moral obligation to *share* these words with you. There is true magic in togetherness. For whatever reason, you have been brought to this, you are now to be given this awareness too and thank you for being open to receive it. When you learn to harness your light through discovering your life purpose and become the best version of yourself, you will truly transform your own life, and this will impact on those around you too. You have your own light within you. Maybe you just don't know it yet. But you will.

Each of us has a story to tell and the world deserves to hear it. Become the author of your own life. – GS

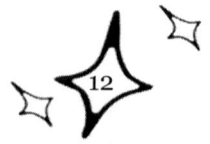

Your journey begins now...

The Light Within You

Discover the power you've always had

Gemma Smith

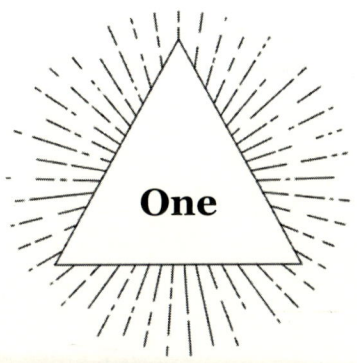

Enlightenment

Enlightenment – the words inside this chapter will open up your mind to what your life art may be and how this can transcend into a beautiful, ever-lasting legacy.

Your craft

There is a plan for each and every one of us. Have you ever felt that there is something bigger and greater than you? That there is a plan waiting to manifest that is much larger than you? We each have a higher purpose and I truly believe that we've been put on this planet for a reason. To fulfil a mission. To manifest a purpose. To serve others and to give back. To give more than we take. We all have something that deep down we want to achieve, whether we know it right now or not is a different matter. But there is something inside each and every one of us – almost like a burning desire waiting to evolve – and while it might take you a long time to find your purpose and although you might not know it now, when you do it will be life-transformational and empowering to a whole new level.

The Light Within You

Your purpose may have the ability to change lives and potentially change the world. Who's to say that your purpose is not great enough to impact the lives of many people? You can be, do and have whatever you want in this world, you just need to believe in yourself and your capability. A dream can never manifest if you don't act, though. Have faith. Act and derive from a place of Love in all that you do. This greater power, as you know it, (which may be God for you as it is for me) wants you to feel safe, it wants you to feel secure and it wants you to radiate that light that is within you. Listen to your inner guidance system. If you can find what it is you truly desire to accomplish in your life, you can start to use your internal light to your advantage. We can have anything that we want in life, we just need to have the right mindset in order to achieve it. We need to put one foot in front of the other.

If you're not currently sure what your higher purpose is, spend a moment thinking about all of the things that make you happy and all of the things that you like to do. Consider if there is a way that you can make what it is that you love doing something that you can be being paid for. For example, I know that I really like to write. When I lived in Spain between 2007 and 2013, I was writing out of pleasure. I knew that I really enjoyed it, but at the time I didn't know how I could make money from it. Yet, I kept trying, I kept fighting and I kept asking people, 'I have this hobby, how do I make money from it?' Eventually, I was given the inspiration from a beloved family member of mine and this allowed me to pursue my dream; write for publications and get paid for writing. My passion was so fierce, and it was that which was able to guide me in the right direction. My internal force protected me, guided me and gave me the strength that I needed to be strong and confident in confronting people, which is not always easy. I just knew that the way writing made me feel wasn't a mere coincidence, it was a signal and it happened for a reason.

When I moved back from Spain, I decided to go to the University of Westminster and chase my purpose. I wanted to understand the art behind writing even more. What matters is that you don't allow anybody else dictate your purpose to you, because you are an individual and you have the choice to decide what you want out of your life and how you want to live it (with the help and guidance from the Higher Power). Of course, we have to be there for others, and we have to take other people's opinions into consideration, but this is your life. You need to take ownership over your life. Sometimes we have to be selfish in order to be selfless and to become the best version of ourselves. It starts from within and be reassured that there is an inner force operating inside of you, it is there for you. Always.

There is a light within you that can be utilised to truly magnify your craft, the art of your life. If you're feeling the struggles and challenges of life, just know that something better and incredible is waiting for you on the other side. Build power from the pain. Sometimes you may think that you are not getting what you want, and you may feel frustrated, but it's because you haven't been asking the right questions. How many times do you sit and ask for something or thank yourself for everything that you have? How much time do you spend talking to your Higher Power? Quiet, alone time talking to yourself and being self-reflective can help you feel reassured. Consciously reflecting may allow you to feel that you are being clear and transparent about your life and the choices that you are making. It allows you to open up those feelings that have been hidden away for a very long time. Unless you are doing something that touches your light, you'll never be able to utilise it fully.

Empower you, empower others

Being the best version of ourselves can sound quite tricky but actually it is something that you too can do. Although you may not know it yet, there are ways that you can bring out the best in yourself. By now, you have thought about something that you enjoy doing and now it's time to consider how that makes you feel and how does it make you act?

It could be that you enjoy dancing, or you may like reading books and when you do those things it brings out the light in you. The flames ignite. It makes you feel good. I know that if I'm driving home from a hard day's work at school, being a teacher, if I play some of my favourite songs it can help to put me in such a great spirit. In that moment, I am happy, I am liberated. It doesn't matter how I felt prior to that, the moment I play a song I adore or the moment I think about the words in the song that truly resonate with me, it automatically lifts me up. Out of nowhere I become the best type of me. You must do those things that enable you to rejoice; for you to feel a sense of peace and joy in your heart.

So, think about the things that you enjoy and what puts a smile on your face. Intentionally strive to

Enlightenment

bring out the best of your personality, of your energy, of all that you are. You owe that to the world and people want to see you happy, people want to feel your incredible energy and life that you have to share with others. Each and every one of us are unique and we need to humbly recognise that and celebrate our talents and achievements every now and then. It's important to give back to our self.

Life can be difficult. We go through many stages where we are faced with hardships that can often tear us apart and temporarily destroy our emotions. It's not easy and nobody said it would be, but you have to find the motivation from within *you* to get yourself out of the emotional turmoil you may be in. When you feel yourself getting upset or torn apart, just think to yourself 'I need to take some control, this needs to stop. I deserve better. This is not fair on me and it is not fair on those around me.'

Whatever it is you have to do, no matter what others think or say, follow it through and listen to your heart, to the voice inside of you, the Higher Power guiding you. If it makes you happy and gleam with joy, do it. When you are happy, you are sending out positive vibes, which are contagious and can potentially affect those around you in a positive way. Happiness spreads, just like when you smile at somebody and they smile back at you. People catch on to warm, uplifting energy and that is why serving others, sharing your innate warmth with others, is so significant. Now, there is a true power in being somebody who makes people *think and feel*. People might look at you differently and think, 'Wow, how has this person made me feel this

The Light Within You

way? How have they done that to me? They've made me think about things in a way that I didn't know was possible.' This can happen just by you empowering yourself... giving back to you in order to empower and give back to others. Once you are empowered and fired up, you are then in a position to be able to do that to other people and bring out the best in others and any situation. I have found in my life that when I do something kind for somebody else or when I say kind words to others, it makes me feel alive inside. It makes me feel like the inner force has put me on the right path, I'm doing what I should be doing and I'm being a decent, wholesome human being.

I think a lot of us can forget what it means to be a human sometimes, being in the present moment and connecting with others. Connectivity in the present moment can be taken for granted, especially with the ever-growing distraction of technology at our fingertips. It can be easy to forget to appreciate the little things and be grateful for what you do have; what are the 'happenings' around you at the moment that you can observe, admire and be a part of? We can be so busy thinking about the past or the future that we totally dismiss and fail to recognise the very present moment. The very moment that is promised to us; in the here and now.

If you see somebody struggling, help them. What words can you say to a person that may be in a dark place that will make them feel better, more hopeful about the future? How can you help them to perhaps see things differently, in an alternative way, from a more optimistic perspective? Can you help somebody see the good in a bad situation?

Isn't life full of lessons, teaching us, equipping us to make us stronger, worthier and wise? There are always alternatives and sometimes, people are just trapped in their own mind. They're waiting for that inspiration, for that glimmer of hope. You can be the one to give them what they may be searching for. Always give more than you take; after all, we are here to serve others, to give back and provide love and service for our brothers and our sisters. This is what gives humanity true purpose and peace.

Vulnerability is an opportunity

I know the power of opening up because I have been in many situations where I have felt uncomfortable talking about something in particular and being around an environment that I didn't agree with, but I found that once I pushed through those uncomfortable moments, it made me feel free. I felt that sense of freedom and a sense of joy that I didn't know existed. Serenity. Opening up to people, especially the ones that you love, can really help you to connect with them on a deeper level. You may find that they understand the things that you thought they wouldn't, and if they don't, you learn from the experience. I didn't know that there was that possibility.

Being vulnerable can really open up a lot of opportunities as it can allow us to connect and establish ourselves with someone in an emotional way. Vulnerability is essential for relationship building. Don't travel along in life being in your own comfort zone, thinking that it's okay to let life pass by without anyone else being a part of your beautiful journey. As I say in the classroom, 'teamwork makes the dream work' and building intimate connections with others is a blessing. There are so many people that may feel the way that you do, that are just waiting for you to open up, so that they can open up in return.

Why don't you initiate? Why not spark the flame? Sometimes you just need to be the person that leads by example. Watch the power that opening up has on others, as it can really bring out something special, something that the person has been hiding and keeping enclosed for a long time. Once you have said 'listen' or 'I need to tell you something' or 'can I just get your opinion on this?' you will be amazed at how many people invite your vulnerability, how easy it feels to initiate and connect.

They want to hear what you have to say. They want to feel what you're feeling. They want to empathise with you. Many of us find it very difficult to face our fears but it can be very enlightening. Yet it's easier said than done and I have been in many situations where I have felt afraid to see something through. For example, when I went travelling at the age of 19, I decided to do a sky dive in Australia. I knew that I could, and I would, so I decided to spontaneously book the sky dive without much thought. I knew the more I thought about it, the more reasons I'd come up with for not seeing it through. Even though I wasn't doing it that day, I knew that it was booked and there was nothing I could do about it. At times, you just need to face your fears without thinking too hard about the fear itself. The longer the wait continues, the harder the concrete fear lives within you. It can throw your mind in all sorts of directions, it can cause so much anxiety, procrastination and ultimately, prevent you from doing something you desire... that is *not* fair on you. Don't think about it, just DO it.

Legacy – make your mark

In order to be enlightened and enlighten others, you need to think about your legacy. Think about your art – that something you absolutely love doing – how you empower yourself, how you empower others and being vulnerable in the process, and ask yourself 'How do I want to make my mark on the world?'

How do you want to be remembered? How do you want other people to think of you? Everything that you do, are and say has consequences. Reactions are caused by actions – all of your actions have meaning, they are all felt by other people and all of the things you do amount to something bigger, something greater. You may not realise it yet, but all that you do towards achieving your dreams or towards doing something great contribute towards your final result, your destination. It may take a very long time but eventually you will get there. It's about the journey and enjoying every step, every milestone of achievement. Believe in yourself!

For me, I know that I want to be remembered in a way that makes people think brightly about life, optimistic for a promising future. You may want to be remembered for something that cannot be seen but felt. Or you might want to be remembered for being an expert in your field, and again, that's incredible because it's completely unique to you and your life path, your life art. Everything works together in alignment to help you achieve pure enlightenment in order for you to design, create, share and impact upon others. There is true power in being the designer of you own life, in taking control. If you want to become an artist, for example, design your own masterpiece in your private time, whether you're busy at work or not, don't give up and dismiss it altogether. Find the time to invest in you! It's so easy to put your own self last on the agenda but how is that going to be beneficial to you and what you can offer and serve to others in the future? *'Time is like a river. You cannot touch the same water twice, because the flow that has passed will never pass again. Enjoy every moment of your life.'* – Be positive be happy.

Take back the power that you've always had inside of you. Share your wisdom and your mark. We all have wisdom and something valuable to share with others. We each live our own lives and have built a wealth of knowledge and experiences in a way that nobody else has. You and I see things differently and that's beautiful. We are all individuals and we cannot expect other people to be, think and act the way that we think is right. There is power in collaboration and in being at one with other people, sharing our true purpose and being mindful to celebrate that. Celebrating our own success may inspire another person's success. Isn't that a gift? Each milestone that you achieve towards reaching your dream needs to be appreciated because otherwise life will just pass you by. Be present and be proud, even if it is a small amount of progress you have made. Don't be mad at yourself for not doing as much as you had intended or for not succeeding with your original intentions. Keep that hope and faith alive in the power and impact you can have on others and let that be the driver, let

Enlightenment

that empower you and become your '*why*' factor. How great would that make you feel to know you have left something valuable behind for others to benefit from?

It doesn't matter where you are right now, it's never too late. It may be that you leave your house and you say hello to somebody who looks lonely or you help someone who has dropped their bag. Be the helping hand that a lot of us need. Take back that power that you've always had. There is a plan for you. You need to find it, you need to utilise it, and it will be much more powerful when you shine your inner light onto your art and your truest purpose. So, ask yourself, how do *you* want to be remembered?

Discover the light within you to gain the strength to make a change. A change that matters to you. – GS

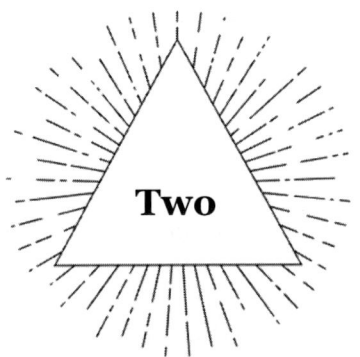

Purpose

We all have a purpose – harness the power of your voice, your individuality and the spirit that lives within you, while understanding yourself on a deeper level. Gain a true clarity of 'self'.

Your voice, your why

Everybody on this planet has their own voice; a voice that is destined to come out and to be heard (literally or felt through communication). You and I each have messages that can be shared with other people because we both have different life experiences. We may not know what that message is straight away, and we may not feel that we have completely found our voice, but it will come, over time, with self-confidence, self-belief and learning how to truly harness your internal light. As an individual, we hold our own internal morals, values and belief systems and this can shape who we are, how other people see us and where we decide to go in life.

When we decide to keep our voice inside of us, hidden from the world, we are in fact prohibiting the truth to come out. We are suppressing our own truths. It may be that the people around you desperately want to hear your truth and could benefit greatly from what you have to say. The problem is, is that most of us are scared of what people think. We are fearful of being judged and of being thought about in a way that we're not comfortable with. Let's get rid of that belief system. Now!

You have to learn to be comfortable in your own skin, whether there are consequences or not, is irrelevant. If you are not being true to yourself, how do you expect to move forward in your life? How do you expect to find serenity? You cannot progress as an individual, if you are restricting yourself from being who you really are. When you find your voice, it can be truly life transforming. You will start to notice people noticing you more. Maybe you have always hidden in the corner and was afraid to really stand out but that won't be the case anymore. You might be thinking 'I don't like to stand out' but never forget that you are ultimately still in control of what is and what can be, but what matters most is that you are always being true to yourself. Don't suppress your extraordinary internal energy, that glowing light inside of you. Be you because you are amazing, and you matter.

What is your why? To help you realise who you really are as an individual, it can be helpful to figure out what matters most to you. When you are motivated by something in particular, it may feel as though nothing else matters because you have a bigger, more meaningful purpose at stake. When you can dig deep into your heart and soul (brainstorm if you have to, by jotting down all the things you deeply love), you may be able to unleash

Purpose

what it is that really means the most to you. Pinpoint those things and strive for them. Depend on them to see you through when times get tough and challenging.

For example, I am a Primary School Teacher and when I am having a hard, challenging day, I remember my *'why'*. My *'why'* is that I am there for those children, the children are what matter the most to me in my profession and ensuring that I can give them the best possible education and opportunity to thrive. When I am in a difficult situation or feeling a sense of stress I stop and think about my *'why'* and all of sudden, the moment of hardship suddenly doesn't feel half as bad. Thinking about those children and how much they deserve the best version of myself enables me to move forward, to look ahead instead of looking back. The whole world makes sense again as though the missing pieces of the puzzle are arranged back together.

If you don't know what you *'why'* is, make a list of all the things that are important to you and then focus on one in particular. Ask yourself, which one feels right? What one stands out the most to you? Then, you can write that *'why'* down or install it firmly into your mind so that it is going nowhere. You may not use or refer to it some days, and that'll be because you won't need to, but when you do feel a drop in your emotions or when you are feeling low, it'll be there ready in your locker to depend on and get you through a challenging time. Remember *'why'* you're doing something, make it purposeful and keep looking ahead.

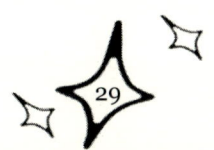

Control your mind

Staying in control of your mind is important if you want to become successful but that is definitely easier said than done, especially in the world that we live in where so much is going on all of the time.

We have become a race of distraction, constantly doing things to distract our minds from what '*is*'. It is hard and rare to shut off and to then be okay with the silence or to be okay in the present moment. When I was younger I was taught an important lesson and it has stuck with me throughout my life; '*we must learn to stay in control of our mind instead of letting our mind control us*'.

When we let our minds control us it is as though we are letting our subconscious minds run on 'auto-pilot', without any control from us or our conscious minds. Is it okay that we lose control over our SELF? Absolutely not. The key to being in control of your mind is to be in the present moment.

I completely understand that it is a hard thing to do, because I struggle with it myself. It can be easier to sit on a train scrolling through our phone instead of looking up and appreciating what is going on around us. I do it a lot, especially when I am walking, I forget to take in what is going on around me. It actually makes me feel empty inside when I reflect upon it. We know it's not right but what shall we do? How can we change that mindset?

Increasingly it is being suggested that we can consciously improve our mindset by simply being more careful about what content we consume

Purpose

because our input and output are intrinsically linked.

> Input=Output – What you decide to ingest on a daily basis has a profound effect on you and the way you think about things.

For example, when I was younger, I used to be naughty by watching some horror movies that I shouldn't have seen because I was considered too young to watch them. Without realising it at the time, watching those movies had a long-term effect on my mental health. To this day, I am a very frightened person.

Although I have adopted the *'feel the fear but do it anyway'* approach, I still learned that what I put in, I get out. What I watch has an impact on my life and this is something we should all be aware of. When thinking about our purpose and where we want to go in life, we need to be mindful of our input.

We need our input to enrich us, reawaken our souls and spark the flames to our internal light and that can mean curating the kind of content that we consume.

If I want to feel happy and be a happy person for my friends, my loved ones or for the strangers around me, then I need to digest positive material in a conscious, purposeful way. If I am putting negative information inside of me then I am putting myself into a position that I am likely going to execute negative thoughts, conversations and actions. What I put into myself – my mind – will

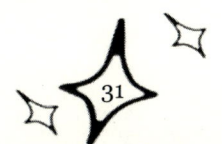

have an ultimate consequence, there *will be* a reaction from it.

So, think about the input you want to put in and consider what do you want to get back from it? What impact do you want that to have on your mindset? You could read a really interesting book, for example, and then share that insightful knowledge with other people by lifting them up and making others feel good. By educating yourself you are widening your horizon, stretching your know-how and ultimately, growing in wisdom and strength.

Gain clarity

Gaining clarity on what you want may seem harder than it is, as I have found that when I stop for a moment within the business of life, I have time and space to think properly and breathe. Consciously breathe and feel the breath flowing in and out of your body.

In doing this, I am able to truly capture clear thoughts in my mind, something that can be hard to do when there is so much going on around you. To find your vision or to gain clarity on your vision, it is important that you take some time for *you*. Allow yourself time to think, whether that means being alone, or being around others who stimulate your thoughts and give you ideas. Ultimately, do whatever works best for *you*.

Pinpointing your life vision is essential to move forward because once you have gained clarity on what your vision is you can then put the steps in place to help you get there. For example, if you have

Purpose

decided that you want to become a professional swimmer, and that is something you really want to do with your life, from that thought you can then start attending swimming lessons. Or you might decide to seek advice from other professional swimmers on social media because <u>association breeds similarity</u>. <u>Surround yourself with the people that inspire you, that are within the circle of success that you wish to enter.</u>

I believe that the people who you associate with can greatly impact the person you become, so if you want to be a professional swimmer, learn from them, associate with them and let one be your role-model. Reach out and seek what you need. Don't forget to communicate with the Higher Power consistently and listen for the response. The light within you is a part of you, after all.

> The manifestation of a particular idea cannot happen if you are not clear on what it is that you want.

My outlook on life hasn't changed, it has just been strengthened. My brain is more fixed than it ever was before. Dedication, motivation and a desperation to become better; worthier for others. I believe that there is no better satisfaction than achieving something you previously thought of as totally out of your reach; you learn through pain, through stepping away from the 'comfort zone' and from feeling a fear of doing something but doing anyway (because you know in your heart that either way, it is a win because you will ultimately learn from the experience).

The Light Within You

To achieve a lot of things in life there needs to be a sacrifice. You have to set things aside for a while to allow yourself time and space to harness your energy on something more important. After all, it may be something much bigger than yourself, something that has the power to change your life and the lives of those around you. So, be a bit ruthless and be responsible for what truly counts and don't sit around and wait for it to happen. A dream will only remain as a dream if you choose to not act.

When you express yourself in the way that you feel is right, something magical can happen. You may learn something about yourself that you didn't know before. Life is busy for the majority of us, and much goes on that makes it hard for us to stop and express ourselves. Being creative opens up the unique part of your mind that allows you to think differently about things and situations. You put yourself in a position whereby you open new doors and you are open to new possibilities. Sometimes it's necessary to not think too deeply about expressing yourself. It could be as simple as jotting down your thoughts or writing a poem about something that matters to you. Or talking to a close friend.

Thinking *'outside the box'* as a lot of people like to call it gives you a cutting edge. It's almost as if you gain a sense of individuality, you have a power to be original compared to other people. The power to be entirely and uniquely you. When you are living in a moment of expressing yourself, you have a profound ability to find answers to problems that you didn't have before. Focus on the solutions.

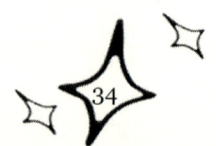

For example, if I am at school planning for one of my whole class reading lessons and I am stuck for ideas, I decide to be creative by brainstorming different tasks and activities that the children can do. I free my mind for a moment and I just '*be*' in the present moment, I avoid distractions and I shut off from the world. I pick up a pen and a piece of paper and I think about all of the things that have been done already and then out of nowhere, I am able to identify gaps. Once the gap has been identified, I am able to create something new but then I think of ways that it can be delivered in a real fun and interesting way. To do this effectively, I might look for inspiration on the internet or I might use something I have done already that I can recreate in a new way and with new content. Being creative doesn't always mean that it has to be an original idea. Someone close to me always says: *'take what's been done and accept what's useful, reject what's useless and add specifically your own unique ideas'*. This concept alone has really helped me to not be afraid of expressing myself as I know that from somewhere, usually within quiet time, answers will be born.

Master of self

Believe it or not, you have the power to be, do and have whatever it is you want in this world. What is missing is that you may not be asking for it, you may not be in full alignment with the inner force and you may not be currently mastering yourself. You may not be asking the right questions to the Higher Power or searching for the right guidance. Have you ever just sat there and thought: who am I?

The Light Within You

Over time I have come to realise that you are what you think you are. Whether it's true or not is irrelevant. Self-fulfilling prophecy means that whatever is said to you or whatever you yourself affirm, regardless of whether it is true or not, becomes your own personal truth.

The more frequently you affirm something to yourself, the more likely it is going to be that you believe it. When you believe something, it has an effect on your entire being.

For example, if somebody calls you a nasty name and they continue to call you that name over and over again, you may start to believe it to be true and when you do, what could be the consequences? You will likely have a low self-esteem and a lack of confidence. You will probably not believe in yourself very much and if anybody tries to say something kind to you, you're likely to dismiss it and reject it because you won't feel worthy enough.

The lesson here is to be careful what you choose to believe. Don't let other people's opinion become your reality. Talk to yourself, to your inner child, to your soul. Healing is not something you can find externally, it is already *within you* and so, healing has to come *from you*. From the inside out.

Remember that every person in this world has their own opinion, it doesn't necessarily mean that their opinion is right, fair or true. They have lived their own life and they have endured their own experiences; it is their voice and therefore it is their truth and not yours.

Purpose

A realisation which has always been very powerful for me is the idea that if somebody says something negative towards you, it says a lot about them but nothing about you. It's like a mirror with their reflection looking back at them, showing a person who may be emotionally traumatised. Instead of feeling angry or hurt by what they have said, always wish them well and bless that they will find their own strength to escape their suppressing thoughts and words. If they are happy to put themselves in a position where they are radiating negative words and are willing to put people down or make people feel bad, what does that tell you about them as a person? It is that person's problem to deal with and not yours. So, don't listen to other people in such an obeying way, be critical and think critically. Be the master of your own mind and be in control of your own choices.

You have all the power you need to become the person you want and urge to be, and it's all already inside of you. Once you have realised your *true purpose*, found your *voice*, your *why* and can see clearly what your vision is, then you will feel empowered. You will have the opportunity to showcase this sense of realisation with other people. You will be able to shine bright, well and truly, like the stars in the night sky. People all around you will feel and sense your contagious, positive force of energy and in turn they will want to be around you and follow your footprints.

Encourage the delivery of positive affirmations to *yourself*. For example, on my wall in my bedroom I display mine and read them every day. 'I am confident. I am powerful. I am strong. I am a giver. I am a leader. Be grateful.' Your mantras, what you

The Light Within You

say to yourself consistently, need to live within you and drive you forward to that special place of self-belief. Feel alive and empowered to be who you are and undoubtedly, be proud of it. Be thankful. Remember, there is only *one* you and you are lucky enough to have the light within you that is guiding you every single day. Trust in your light...

You may wish you had known 'this' or known 'that' but ask yourself, if you had known, would you have done things differently or should it have just been that way? Trust your light to shine bright in the present moment and accept what is to be enough because your light is your only way. – GS

Bigger Than You

Bigger than you – ever wondered how you can infectiously spread love among others? The biggest way to help yourself is to help others.

Spread a smile

I have a philosophy that I truly believe in; you should spread a smile wherever you go and whenever you can. Have you ever walked down the street feeling really lonely and miserable and then out of nowhere, a stranger decides to smile at you? How did that make you feel when that happened? Great, I bet. There is true power in the little things in life. Those little things that you can do for others without much effort at all.

So many of us take the little things for granted or fail to see them, let alone acknowledge the true impact that they have. If you are able to spread joyous behaviour with others, you are being a true light in their life (even if it is only for an instant). The smile that you can give someone may be just what that person needs in that very moment of despair, stress or anger. It may be the missing piece to the puzzle that they have been yearning for and it might be all that is needed to make them feel okay again. I have noticed that when I smile at a stranger, it actually makes me feel good, too. It doesn't just have a positive effect on the person on the receiving end, it has a positive effect on the giver. Giving makes us feel good. Giving lifts us up and makes us realise that there is more to life than ourselves. It makes us feel alive and reminds us that we have a purpose. Once we have mastered our self and feel in a position to share our best self with others (which some people may mistakenly deem as being selfish), you can then offer your beautiful attitude and energy with others (that is what would be considered as being selfless). When you have reached this point, you are shining from a place of love, you are shining from a place of certainty, peace and innate serenity.

Now, don't get confused, I know it can be hard to maintain this level of empowered positivity all of the time and that's completely understandable (because as we said, life can be difficult and can throw us several unexpected challenges). But what counts is how we react and that we start by recognising, acknowledging and appreciating the little things to help ground ourselves.

When we feel our moods or emotions drop, we need to consciously try and lift ourselves back up again because we have to be intentional with our input and output. We have to be purposeful with our words and what impression we want to create. All of the little things DO matter, and it can start with a simple offering of a smile to a stranger. That small gesture can make your day and give you a sense of purpose. By paying more attention to the little things, you may find that it impacts upon the bigger things in your life, for example, your overall attitude and sense of comfortability in a social setting. If you are focusing on being a good person by smiling or holding the door open for strangers, you are embedding kindness into your being. It is becoming a part of you and you are consciously designing your humanly ways to make it become even more concrete and real.

If you are spreading warm and positive energy, you are sending out the signal that you are at one with others. You are not separate or on this journey alone. You are riding this journey, called life, with millions of other people and with the Higher Power within your heart. Lifting other people up is a liberating experience and has an incredible ability to make us feel good, to feel worthy of something much greater. When we feel good, what happens? Magical things around us start to happen because we are on the right track. Do whatever you can to *feel* good. The simple act of sharing a smile just may do the trick.

Be the change

Something that has become clearer to me as I have got older, is that we cannot change the actions and behaviours of other people. Life can feel quite tough and frustrating when those around us are saying things that we don't agree with, especially if they are loved ones. Something that I have realised is that I am not that person. Those around me are on their own life journey, they are on their own path and their path is not my path. I cannot force other people to do what I want them to do or to do what I believe is right. Whether I like it or not, those around me that I love are going to do what they want regardless of what I say or think. I had a realisation that if I want to have a positive influence on other people, I just need to be the change that I want to see. I need to shine my light and be the best version of myself to hopefully inspire and enlighten other people to follow my direction. It doesn't matter what I say or how I go about saying it because they are on their own life path and it is for those individuals to learn and grow in their own personal way that is right for them. There is nothing wrong with wishing the best for somebody, however, unrealistic expectations attract disappointments. You can't force people to do anything, no matter how much you believe in what you're trying to do. The inner force is with those individuals all of the time, trying to show them the way while guiding and protecting them. By demonstrating and showing the way to unleash the light from within, you will have more of a chance of bringing out the best in others. Have faith.

Leading by example is powerful; you have an ability to set the tone and set the standard whoever you are around and in any social environment. Have you ever been around other people that gossip, talk about other people or constantly moan or complain? Yes, probably many times. Now, think about how it makes you feel afterwards. Have you ever sat there and felt physically, mentally and emotionally drained, but you don't know why? See, people have the power to affect your energy which is why it is so crucial that we strive to protect it. If you are around conversations that suppress feeling at peace, calm and balanced, either try and switch it up and talk about something different or find the serenity from within you to maintain your calm. *Learn* from the experience and see it as a *lesson*.

Lessons are all around us, but it is whether we consciously choose to absorb them or reject them without realising. When I was at university, I struggled with this concept a lot. I really enjoyed socialising and being around other people. I enjoyed engaging in conversations and listening attentively. After all, I was taught that it is much more powerful to be a good listener, instead of being a good talker.

When you listen, you have the potential to learn and absorb new information, which means you can grow in knowledge and wisdom. When you talk you are just affirming what you already know, meaning you have less chance of growing in knowledge. For me, comprehending and digesting this concept has been difficult because whilst I understand that it is essential to listen and converse, I sometimes struggle to protect my own energy in uncomfortable situations.

At times, I would much rather be alone and protect my thoughts, than potentially damage them with the gossiping words of others. Now, there needs to be a careful balance in these situations because sometimes, people are stuck in a place that they need saving from and you have the potential to do that by shining your light onto them. But I think we, as human beings, are a good judge of character. I bet you are able to tell if someone just thrives off gossip and talking badly about someone or whether or not that person is genuinely in a dark place and needs a shoulder to lean on. Like I said before, you are your own master with your own flickering light living within you. Believe in your own judgement, your spiritual guidance system, and always aim to lead by example. Come from a place of love and you'll seldom go wrong.

The beauty in giving

There can be huge satisfaction and gratification in giving to others, a true beauty that a lot of people often underestimate. There is a Chinese saying that goes: '*If you want happiness for an hour, take a nap. If you want happiness for a day, go fishing. If you want happiness for a year, inherit a fortune. If you want happiness for a lifetime, help somebody.*' For a long time, the greatest thinkers have suggested the same thing: happiness is found in helping others. When you give from the heart, from a sincere place of love, you are offering something to somebody else. When you give, you are in a place of being able to receive in return because '*what goes around comes around*'. I witness these moments a lot but when I say give, I don't always mean giving through materials and money. Giving can mean giving someone your time, a valuable gift granted to us that is infinitely precious. Giving someone your eye-contact, to show respect. Giving someone a smile, to warm their spirit. Giving someone a helping hand when they look stuck. Giving someone a shoulder to cry on, when that person has shut down emotionally. Giving someone that glimmer of hope, through a word or two. Giving comes in many different forms and it depends on the context in which you give and how you apply it. True fulfilment comes when you invest in something much *larger than yourself.*

I am currently the Global Goodwill Ambassador Chair for the UK on LinkedIn. I have worked tirelessly on reports for the organisation and created nominations during my free time. I review applications and conversate with people all over the world. I don't get paid for doing this, I do it because I love to collaborate with other humanitarians and be a part of something much greater than myself. It gives me satisfaction and joy in a way that material objects can't give. I also have a *'yes'* mindset and attitude whereby if any member of my family calls upon me for any help or support (with absolutely anything), I will strive to do my absolute best to help them, no matter the situation I'm in. There is a real power in the personal growth that you can gain when you give to others. Being selfless and giving service to others in need will gift you internally:

For it is in giving that we receive — Saint Francis of Assisi

The sole meaning of life is to serve humanity — Leo Tolstoy

We make a living by what we get; we make a life by what we give — Winston Churchill

Making money is a happiness; making other people happy is a super happiness — Nobel Peace Prize recipient Muhammad Yunus

Giving back is as good for you as it is for those you are helping, because giving gives you purpose. When you have a purpose-driven life, you're a happier person — Goldie Hawn

Togetherness

Not many people realise that a group of people (a collective) can often accomplish what an individual cannot do alone. There is huge power and potential in teamwork. When you collaborate with other people, you are allowing yourself to learn from other people, share your ideas with other people and potentially team up in different avenues. Togetherness is important. Perhaps not all of the time, because alone time is also crucial to develop your own ideas, develop your voice and get closer to your true purpose. Balance is key.

Yet coming together with others should not be underestimated, nor should it be something that we are afraid of. It can be daunting joining a team of people or coming together with complete strangers. For example, I have been to a lot of networking events and there is normally that moment when you are asked to go and speak to strangers in the room. My heart pounds, my eyes move all around the room (desperately trying to avoid direct eye contact) and I try to keep myself busy to avoid it. The true power of procrastination (wanting to put it off). Why have I done that? It may feel scary speaking to people that you don't know but the truth is, you should embrace any opportunity to talk to someone new. Embrace opportunities that offer the chance to share, listen and come together (in whatever context that may be). There is certainly no I in the word TEAM is there? Really and truly *'teamwork makes the dream work'* because you are working together to achieve the same goal. Working together can reap incredible, life-transforming results. You might just be the person that the other person needs and wants to collaborate with to make their dream a reality, and in doing so you may uncover truths about yourself that you never knew were possible to achieve. You may just reveal a *hidden gem*.

Contact, Care, Collaborate. What do I mean by that? In order to achieve great '*togetherness*', you need to find the strength and willpower to contact someone new. Whether that is contacting someone in the same room as you, sending that important person an email or text, making a brave phone call or going out of your way to visit somebody that you know you need and want to. There can be a slight cross-over when it comes down to deciding: do I need to contact that person? Do I want to contact that person? Either way, both are important. Whether you want to or need to, just do it! Feel the fear but go for it anyway.

Once you have made that initial contact with someone (it may even be with the one you love or a close friend), you then need to show a sense of care. When you show signs of being a caring person, you are opening up the door for that person to connect with you. Connection is essential. We are all human beings and we are all in this together. So, open your arms to connect. Don't hold yourself back or restrict yourself from connecting as when you do, you ignite the light of *connection*. You may have felt it before when you connected with somebody that you never knew, and you felt alive afterwards. You felt intrigued and inspired just by being around another incredible being.

Once you have reached this level of communication, you are then in a position to collaborate. It is very difficult, in fact it is extremely challenging, to collaborate with someone who you haven't contacted nor showed any signs of *caring* about them. Why would someone want to collaborate with you if you don't contact or show that you care? It's practically and humanely impossible to expect.

The Light Within You

Even if it is with a loved one and you're thinking about the togetherness in that sense, if you haven't shown any *love* towards them (way deeper than displayed affection) then it is a problem to collaborate on a deeper level of communication. True light will shine between people once they open up, display vulnerability and operate from a place of love.

Decide you want your dream more than it scares you and let that be your ultimate 'why'. – GS

Four

Rise Up
Rise up – do you yearn to know how you can push through boundaries and limitations that you set yourself? Explore the beauty in striving for more, seeing more of this world and growing spiritually in the process.

Everyone has a mountain to climb

When I set out on my own mission to climb a mountain, the '*Roof of Africa*', I never expected that I would actually reach the top of the summit. When I booked my trip, it was quite a spontaneous decision and I had no idea what I was in for. At the time, all I knew was that I was embarking on something bigger than I had ever done in my entire life. Naturally, I had many mixed emotions about it and it is absolutely fine to feel that way, it shows that you are human and that you are pushing your boundaries, and this will ultimately lead to a flourishing growth of strength.

When I first booked my travelling trip I felt a combination of excitement and being overwhelmed. It brought back nostalgic memories of how I felt when I went travelling in 2012. On that occasion I visited Thailand, Malaysia, Singapore, Australia and New Zealand, all of which I did by myself. If I was to describe jetting off alone like that it would be through the sense of *freedom* that I felt. Not knowing where you are going, what you will be seeing or whom you may meet, for me, is such an addictive feeling. I first got inspired to travel because I have always been interested in the *bigger picture* – the world around us. We live in this huge place that is free (not literally) to roam around, whether by car, boat, train or plane, as some examples, so why not explore what's out there and discover new things for yourself? Your vision of life becomes instantly widened and broadened by what you learn, see and experience along the way. You may find that the connections which are born along the journey become significant for you and your future, opportunities may even start to present themselves to you too. Sure, going alone is pretty scary, but what isn't nowadays? I say take the risk because every day in this living life is a risk, and what you don't do you will probably regret for the rest of your life.

We need to *rise up*. Together. It's said that we regret things we don't do more than the things we do and if you take a risk, you'll instead have stories to tell about the adventures you decided to embark on, even when you thought they weren't possible at the time. Through reflection you shall see.

Why Mount Kilimanjaro? I have always been extremely fascinated with Africa – it is thought of as the *motherland* and I was keen to have my eyes opened even more through experiencing this sacred place myself. I wanted to learn about the local people and the communities as well as immersing myself in a whole new culture that I had never witnessed before. I questioned different ways of travelling around Africa and I sat back and said to myself, '*I would really love to climb a mountain in my lifetime, a really big one*'. Then I remembered all of the stories a few of my friends had told me about 'Kili' and how incredible it was for them. They said it literally changed their lives, so I wondered how, why, and by what? It got me thinking. Then I thought, why don't I go and experience it all for myself and find out? And that was when I took the *leap of faith*.

We all have fears and we all go through times where we doubt our capabilities, and ourselves, and it is during these hardships we become afraid of what we can achieve rather than what we cannot. That is why I think we all need to face our fears headstrong and use our inner strength, our drive and stubborn determination to spontaneously chase our dreams. There really is no better day than *today*. What are you waiting for? Like I said in the previous chapter, don't think about it too much. Just go for it.

My clear mind, strong mental stamina, positive attitude combined with a fantastic group of people with a fantastic team spirit was – I was certain – what I needed to get me to the top of my mountain climb. When I did triumph, I was alive, I was happy, and I was free. I felt a sense of serenity and inner peace. Did my horizon broaden? Of course, it did, and it was beyond all expectations. Not only did I learn a lot about myself and how great the body is at adapting and fighting through muscle aches and pains, but I also learned a lot about other people and how they deal with things differently to me. And that's absolutely fine. I used all of the detrimental comments and doubts to my advantage. Ultimately, it was all down to *me*. Remember, you have *the light within you*. Let it guide you and show you *the way*.

Travelling is a priceless experience, and what you learn along the way cannot be taught in a classroom or in your hometown.

Risk-taking – live right and look left

'*Live right*' means to live life to the fullest by making sure that you make the most out of any situation. '*Look left*' means that while you are living life to a maximum amount of happiness and fulfilment, always look behind you and check your tracks. Never get up and leave without looking behind you. If you're walking down the street for example, be self-aware. Look around you and ensure that you are always aware of your surroundings, considering the who, what and where.

At times, although you have a light within you, you may find yourself surrounded by darkness, both internally and externally. I like to prepare for the worst outcome before it has even happened, not from a place of fear but from a place of preparation. Some people have disagreed with me on this and said that it is wrong because I'm placing situations in my mind that are not a truth. But for me, it allows me to be completely self-equipped, ready for whatever outcome that life may throw at me. Being ready for the worst means that I am more than prepared to take on challenges, to place myself into uncomfortable spaces and face up to situations that will help me grow.

Rise Up

At the end of the day, you have the capacity to know, be and have so much more. So, how can you grow from staying where you are, from not moving forward or from stopping yourself facing challenges head on?

Yet imagine how much more you can learn by throwing yourself in the deep end and doing things you have always wanted to do but were stopped by limitations. Being adventurous is exciting, maybe not for everyone, but those who break past the fixed mindset and want to get rid of a set routine, adventure is often addictive. It really is about the small things in life: good company, unexpected achievements, being happy, living in the present moment and not alienating yourself from the real world. When I was on the mountain, I was living in the moment and it felt priceless. Love yourself, believe in yourself, follow your intuitions and it will be hard for you to go wrong when you travel. Or in life in general. Enjoy the freedom of travelling with every part of you, feel energised and see the world that we live in because it really is such a beautiful place. Climb a mountain if you have to, it will undoubtedly change your life.

The *yes mindset*– what do I mean? I have found throughout my life that I just cannot help but say yes to things (most of the time). I say yes when people ask for my help, I say yes to new projects (even though I have too much going on already) and I say yes when somebody just wants to talk to me or seek my advice. I have learned that by being this way I am open to new opportunities. Even during the times when it is a difficult decision, I still like to say yes. When I know deep down I'm overworked, and I am aware it's going to be a struggle, I still yes. Saying yes has become an embedded part of my attitude. The way I see it is if you say no, you are closing off any potential opportunity or experience. You never know what is going to come from the small decisions and choices you make. In the past, I have said yes to helping someone with managing their social media for them and from doing so, they have asked me to continue and have paid me for my services. The fact that you have said yes to reading this book means that you are opening up your heart to new knowledge and wisdom that could benefit you in unforeseen ways. You reading this book is a perfect example to the yes mindset. Adopting a *yes* attitude and mindset can be tiring, and you may battle with yourself at times, but look at it in a different way. Do you know what is going to evolve from putting yourself out there? Probably not. Isn't that exciting? You never know what is behind that closed door so be brave, pull the handle and walk on through...

The journey

'*It's about the journey not the destination.*' – You've probably heard this saying a few times throughout your life already, but what does it really mean?

In life, there are moments when you are probably so caught in doing what needs to be done that you forget to pause for a moment, sit in the silence and digest what you are actually achieving. Ask yourself – where is this going to take me? But then forget about the destination and enjoy every step, embrace every milestone that you reach. For example, when I climbed Mount Kilimanjaro, I knew that I hadn't trained properly, and I was relying on pure mental strength to get me through the experience. Before I left, I had spoken to a few of my friends who had already done the climb and successfully reached the summit and I received some of the most valuable advice – *'Remember to look up'*. It took me a while to understand that comment but now it makes a lot more sense.

When we are entirely focused on what we need to do we may start to feel a sense of pressure, and that can be quite scary. By doing so, we put ourselves in the mindset of *just needing to get there* and as a consequence, we miss the small things that we should be giving thanks to along the way. When it was my time to shine and climb the mountain, I took the advice on board. Even though I was struggling, I was out of breath and over-relying on my asthma inhaler to get me through, I would stop and sit on a rock and just look around me for a moment.

Absorbing and appreciating the *moments*, no matter how small they are, can be extremely empowering. Not only do those small snippets enrich your overall experience but they allow you to capture the experience in your mind's eye. They create a vivid connection and emotion to what it is you're actually doing and achieving.

What you will probably find is that those moments when you do just stop, pause and notice what *is*, those will be the times that you poignantly remember throughout your life. Those are the times you chose to be conscious. You chose to be awake. Don't we all need to consciously choose to be awake more often? You are likely going to forget those moments that you are dreading or trying to rush through just to merely reach the destination. Take time for those small snippets, take it *all* in and be proud of your achievements (no matter how trivial they may seem).

Strive, see, grow

What is it that you truly strive for? What is that you really want? Always think back to your *higher purpose*, your *why*. Widen your horizon.

When I think of a horizon, I think of limitless opportunities, doors opening and new experiences waiting on the other side. The concept itself can come in many forms. You may widen your horizon by travelling and exploring the world or it could be by taking a trip to another city in the same country you live in. You might widen your horizon by talking to somebody you don't know and have wanted to approach for a while. Or it could mean that you just go for it one day and do something completely wild, adventurous and out of the ordinary. When you strive for more, you are opening up to your potential for growth and development as an individual. Like I have said, as a human race we tend to think about things way too much and this can cause a lot of stress and anxiety. The more that we think and try to process the less likely we are to actually do it. Our brain may go into *fight or flight* mode, as it is wired to protect us, and it will do all it can to refrain you from entering danger. This means that during moments of opportunity, your brain is weighing up all of the possibilities and consequences. It is thinking *'should I really do this? I can take the easy way out and stay at home instead. I really cannot be bothered. Oh, I'll do it next time.'* When we allow

Rise Up

our mind to control us and we don't take control, it can be massively detrimental.

To stop that from happening, act on impulse. Don't think about things too much, if it *feels* right then that is usually a strong indication that it is so just say yes. What is the worst that can happen? Wouldn't you rather regret the things you have done instead of regretting the things you haven't? Strive for more, to see more, to become more, all of which widen your horizons within this gift of life. The world is an amazing place full of opportunities and things for you to see and do with millions of people waiting for you to meet. The world is yours! Strive, see and grow because you deserve to.

When you do strive, see and grow you are likely going to gain a sense of *freedom*. When I returned from travelling and I was going through some reflection time thinking about my trip and all that I had done, I concluded that travelling for me was *freedom*. It allowed me to be myself and not have to worry about the internal and external reality of my world as much as I usually would. It wasn't that I didn't care about those around me back at home or love them any less, but I was in a powerless situation. I just had to trust in my internal force, my Higher Power, and then know, feel and believe that all would be okay. That gave me a sense of peace. I felt tranquil on the inside and out.

When you adopt the *go for it* mindset and attitude and do something for yourself, I can almost guarantee that you will feel the same sensation. As a human being, it is important that we embrace moments that allow us to *let go*. We forget about reality for a while in order to immerse ourselves in a brand-new experience. Once it is all over, we return but with brand new perspectives and a wave of reborn strength that has been renewed. We can then see things differently because we have made new memories and have new references to go from. You may find that you start to appreciate things that you never usually would, or you strive to give those that you love more time because you have learned the true value of *time* and how much it is worth to those around you, including yourself. You may feel that money and material possessions mean a lot less to you all of a sudden, because what you have just experienced is priceless.

With the era that we all now live in; it has become an exciting time to embrace new opportunities more than ever before. Life has been facilitated for us. We can have and do whatever we need just at the click of our fingertips. Let's not focus on the negatives aspects of technology but instead embrace the newness of possibility in a way that can benefit you and be utilised.

How can you reap the benefits? What can you do or arrange that will offer you a new perspective or a life changing experience?

What an exciting time to be alive right now! Enjoy every step of the journey and take back the power you've always had...

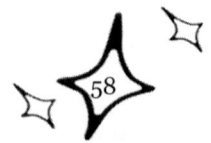

Rise Up

Do the things you know you want to do without any hesitation, it feels right for a reason. It's better to reflect back on what you've achieved than to grow old with regret about the possibilities that you once chose to abandon. – GS

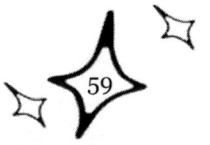

Lifelong Learner

Lifelong learner – cherish education and the life lessons that surround you and use them to your advantage, to better yourself and your soul, while discovering answers in the silence.

Education can change the world

Teaching is a vital part of learning and that is why we're designed to share.
As human rights and apartheid, Nelson Mandela said: *'Education is the most powerful weapon you can use to change the world'*.

Why do I think that's so important? Being an educator, I find it one of the most rewarding professions that is available to humankind. I am passionate about learning and that is why I couldn't get enough of it. I had to teach and work in a learning-based setting. I find that I can teach people purely through my words, just by having a conversation with them and that is why I feel so strongly about education. We need to acknowledge that education is all around us, we can learn from everything that is happening, and in all of the conversations that we have because all of that is

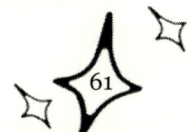

shaping us and building on our thoughts. This creates our internal collection of information, a source that we will return to time and time again throughout our lives. All of those moments you are capturing in your mind's eye, all of those lessons, wherever they may be, are building and developing you as a person.

Sharing is caring – what do I mean by that? Well, being a person that likes to give, I find it extremely empowering to give to others and to share what I have with other people. When I am sharing what I have, whether that be knowledge, an item or a piece of work that I've done that people are interested in, I can see the joy and appreciation in other people's eyes and that is very rewarding. When I am sharing what I know and who I am with people around me, I am opening myself up. I am being vulnerable by giving myself to other people.

By doing this, other people are in a position to be able to do the same in return, through exchanging my wisdom, other people are then inclined to share their inspiration and insight with me. It's a mutual experience, and that means I'm gaining something, I'm growing, I am developing. I am blossoming like a flower as I conversate and share. Having the philosophy or the mindset of *sharing is caring* means that I am choosing a direction of unification (wanting to be in unity with others). In today's world, a lot of people like to keep things to themselves and find it difficult to share what they have and who they are with other people. It may be because they feel afraid that people will become too much like them. Is this the right way to be? Do we choose to be that way, greedy with our knowledge? Or is it because another way hasn't been shown to us? If we haven't been told or shown a new way, then how are we supposed to know?

Children light up my life. They lift me up, they make me smile, they make me feel proud and ironically, they remind me to be a child again. Life can become very routine-like when you're an adult and sometimes we can take life so seriously that it overwhelms us. Life can easily become boring and monotone, especially if we are keeping things to ourselves. There is power in togetherness and opening up to other people.

In my classroom, I strive to make a difference. I strive to open up children's eyes to new possibilities. I don't just rigidly follow the curriculum in a structured way – following the expectations of how lessons should be taught and what the lesson should look like – I use my creative initiative to bring my lessons to life. I try to make them fun, engaging and stimulating. Many of the teachers that I have discussed this with, often feel that by making lessons more fun and engaging it could be distracting for the children who like structure. But I believe that this is a new way of being. Why should we restrict ourselves and what we can offer to the world as a teacher in the classroom or wherever it may be? Isn't it about broadening the minds and imagination of the younger generation? They are the future and deserve to explore this world, and their learning, through creative ways.

There is nothing wrong with using our imagination and taking a risk or showcasing our personal strengths because after all, that could be of a benefit to others. We can use all that is around us to support and empower our children or adults in any setting. No matter where you are or what it is you are doing, try adopting the mindset of being able to make a difference. You can stand out; you deserve to stand out!

As an example, you could be working as a journalist for a high-end newspaper in London and you've been asked to write a particular story that is very interesting, and you could do it vigorously in a very structured format. However, you might decide to deliver the narrative in the form of an infographic and make it even more visually appealing because that's how you would personally like to receive that story and that's the way you envisioned it to be. Trust your intuition. Whatever it is that you are doing, strive to make it as interesting as possible because that way you are likely to stand out above the rest. You can be the one that people will never forget. Be brave.

Life lessons are everywhere

Sometimes you look but you don't see. What do I mean by that? You can be in a particular place where many things are going on around you and it can be overwhelming to the point that you forget to take it all in. You forget to sit there and ask yourself, '*am I present and am I consciously learning?*'

This brings me back to the importance of being in the present moment. People say that meditation is something that should be done alone, in your free time or away from the world but is that entirely true? Somebody close to me has suggested the idea of sitting on the edge of my bed when I wake up in the morning and simply saying the three words, '*am I present?*' Doing this has extreme and infinite power, in fact, it's almost life changing. By consciously sitting and asking yourself the question, you are reflecting, you are being an observer of your own life and thinking about being present. This ensures that you are not being distracted by anything else and not allowing your mind to wander as it usually does. If you start your morning feeling present, it's a feeling that you can then draw on throughout the day, using it to overcome any challenges or decisions that you might face.

Don't underestimate the present moment because being present means that you are being a human being, you are acknowledging, even if it is from a distance, what is going on around you, seeing more of *what is*. We never do anything, we just are, we be, and the doing happens naturally.

Isn't it exciting to know that we are exactly where we are supposed to be? Have faith and trust in the process because there's a bigger plan at play and where you are right now is all part of that journey.

I have found that I am most present when I am in nature, when I am taking a walk outside with my friends, a loved one or it could be when I am on my own and I am simply looking all around me observing the swaying trees, the beautiful blue sky or enjoying the sound of the delicate, chirping birds. In those moments, I am allowing myself to shut off, reconfiguring myself in the right direction – a positive direction – which allows me to take control over my thoughts once again. I no longer feel restricted, trapped or overloaded. That alone

The Light Within You

can transform your day for the better, and it starts with *you* being in *full awareness.*

The value of our childhood

Reflecting on the past can be quite daunting because there might be things that you don't particularly like but that's okay, because there are always things that we are not proud of. There will be moments in your life that you question and doubt, whether or not you should have done it, and that's absolutely fine. Being an observer and reflecting on your past means that you can look back and excrete the life lessons from your childhood. The reflection process is an opportunity to gain something, to learn from the mistakes both you and other people have made, to absorb what was useful and amazing and then you can re-enact that again in your future. Reflecting on your past doesn't always have to be a difficult experience, it can be a journey that you appreciate and invite. This moment now is a gift and that is why it is called the present. Yet, the past is equally important in a different way and it should always be something that we show gratitude for. After all, without it you wouldn't be the person you are today. The past shapes us and makes us stronger. Why not try and utilise the power of the past? Use it to your advantage, don't let it tear you down and break you. Rise above and say, '*thank you, I am learning something from you!*' Why not take back the control? No longer feel afraid to talk about your past or relive the past in your mind. Why does it have to be a bad thing?

When we think about our childhood or our early years, it's really important that we are not too harsh on ourselves and avoid falling into regret over perceived mistakes that we might have made. Instead, it's really important that we realise and accept the mistakes, think about the choices that have been made, and decide to take back power by learning from them as lessons. Embrace the success that can come from the mistakes that you make. See mistakes and regrets as an opportunity to learn, grow and reaffirm to yourself that you will not make the same mistake twice. You can set yourself free and allow yourself to feel alive again.

There are a few ways you can set yourself free from all of the daunting memories that may make you feel stuck, afraid and fearful of the future. You could try writing down all of your mistakes on one side of a piece of paper and on the other side you could write a lesson that you have learned from each mistake. You could keep doing this until you have written out all of the mistakes that create shame and fear inside of you but remember that you always need to make sure that you are thinking about the light that has derived from those dark moments.

That is an example of you taking back the power, discovering the power that you've always had in order to move forward and become a better person. You become an individual that *learns* from the past and doesn't let the past shape or dictate the present moment.

Answers in the silence

Do you appreciate the quiet times? Use it as an opportunity to ask questions and let your thoughts run wild for a moment. It may be useful to get a piece of paper and a pen and write down anything that comes to your mind. Clear that mind of yours that never switches off.

When you write stuff down it helps you to clear your head and free up some space. Time is very important, in many ways, especially when you use it with intention. Everything we do in life, we should try and do it with intention, with a sense of purpose. Think about the reasons and your *w*hy. When you are sitting somewhere, taking time for yourself, have the intention of setting yourself free. Say to yourself, '*I want to clear my mind. Please, give me the answers that I seek. Guide me.*' By saying those words, you are being clear and precise about what you want. Don't just exist, be great! Whatever it is that will make you great, make you feel great or will cause you to become great in a particular area, ask for the answers. Take charge over your mind, your body and your spirit and maintain your calm in situations.

What is the power in meditation and feeling still? When I say the word still, you probably thought I meant that you have to be alone to feel and be still. That isn't quite right. You need to learn to be still even amongst the noise. You need to learn to be in the present moment, even when there is chaos all around you. You may feel that you need healing in many areas, because you feel broken inside about things that have caused you pain and you want fixing. Healing is not something you can find or buy in a shop; true healing starts from *inside of you.* You have a duty to live a happy, fulfilled life and that will mean something different to each and every one of us. All that you are and all that you go through happens to you on purpose. It happens so that you can become the person you need to be. You might be thinking, *'No way. I didn't deserve that. Why me? Why did that happen? I will never forgive that situation.'* True compassion is born when you learn to forgive and let go. Try to comprehend the Serenity Prayer, a prayer that is very meaningful to me and I say it every single day: *God, grant me the serenity to accept the things I cannot change. Courage to change the things I can. And wisdom to know the difference.* Let's break this down further for you to fully understand.

> Accept the things you cannot change: When you are confused about something happening in your life, or feel upset and frustrated, come to terms with it being out of your control and so you could not have done things differently. If it is *you* that is a part of a particular situation, trust in the choices you made at the time. You might have made bad choices, but you did that because you thought it was right at the time. You'll never reach a point of perfection because we are constantly evolving. Learn to accept and let go.

> Courage to change the things I can: If there is something in your life that you are not happy with (it could be your current living arrangement or your profession for example) and you know deep down in your heart you need to change the current situation, but you feel afraid, dig out that strength from within and just go for it. When we are feeling unhappy, that is an indication that we are on the wrong path. We have to trust our inner voice, our instinct some may call it, and we have to respond. When we fail to respond that's when

we choose to ignore change. Change is never easy because we become comfortable with what *is* and sometimes it's much easier to stay where we are and ride through life on autopilot instead of turning our world upside down and changing things. Believe in yourself and the voice inside your head that is trying to offer you a new direction, a direction that will put you on a happier, more fulfilled path.

<u>Wisdom to know the difference:</u> Trust in your ability to know the difference between things you can or cannot change. Respect your judgement.

Believed by most, wisdom comes with age… true power lies in the knowledge of knowing that learning has no age limit. – GS

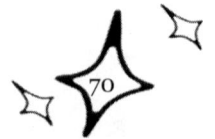

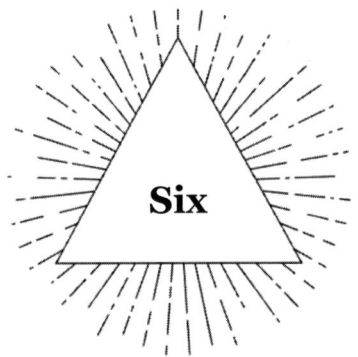

Spread Your Wings

Spread your wings – we can learn a lot through movement as a means of empowering our emotional state. Treasure the divine beauty of nature and learn how to use particular elements to support your wellbeing.

Learn and grow

Alis Volat Propriis is a Latin phrase that translates to '*she flies with her own wings*'. Since I was a little girl, I have always been drawn towards that phrase and although I can't remember where I saw it for the very first time, I do know that it really resonated with me. Why is that?

To me, that phrase means that you have the ability to do anything that you want to do in this world. You are equipped with your own metaphorical *wi*ngs, your own power, your individual internal light that you can use to manifest your dreams and to reach your highest potential. In human terms, the wings are a metaphor for the infinite power that you possess as a human being. What is so magical about those words, and the idea of being able to fly with your own wings, is that they give you back the

power you deserve to have. Those words remind me that I am independent, that I am a worthy individual and that I am worthy of making choices about my life. As are you. Anywhere that you go, go there with belief in yourself and trust that you are being guided by the light that lives within you. You are the light!

When you have a message to give in life, you just know you have to share it with other people. It's like an essential part of you and your being, it's what you were placed on this planet to do and there's no stopping that truth of the matter. No one can tell you otherwise. And no matter how hard you try and fail; the true test of your character will be how quickly you can bounce back from the moments that you felt you had failed.

Growing up I was fortunate enough to get most of the things I wanted from my incredible parents, but times weren't always so easy (for myself). I endured heaps of confusion, unknown answers and challenging moments of doubt about myself as a person and about my journey, but one thing always remained clear, that I loved to write. I took ownership over my identity and I learned to spread my wings as far as I could. To fly off with the pen in my hand and that's still the case to this day. It allows me to express myself, it makes me feel free and liberated from the outside world. A world that can invite so much darkness into my heart. That's why I've learned just how vital it is to know where enjoyment originates from within yourself. Whether that is dancing in the rain, painting on the walls or listening to S Club 7 – whatever it is – it doesn't matter, as long as it makes you happy and can have an encouraging impact on you and your life. Don't forget who you are and never strive for anything less than what you deserve, because you are amazing and there is only one YOU on this planet. You need be the best version of yourself as much as you can.

Motion gives emotion

Inspired by Tony Robin's philosophy *'motion creates emotion'*, it's important to remember that movement and your internal emotions work closely together. They correspond with one another in a perfect ying-and-yang, but this is often something we forget as we move through our lives. Too often we look for the external causes of whatever it is that we are experiencing and fail to understand that often, our feelings and emotions actually come from inside.

Poor functioning and movement of the body can reinforce redundant feelings and emotions. When you decide to change your mental state and break poor habits, you are setting yourself up for a transformation. But movement should be an essential part of this process, as it can truly help you to move forward with your life while creating healthy routines.

There is true power in movement but too many people have got used to being in a sedentary state. This doesn't only slow down their body but sitting still for too long slows down the mind too. When you *stop* for too long you are telling yourself and your brain to *'slow down. I'm not doing much now. There's not much point in thinking too hard, I might as well shut off.'* You stop harnessing your internal power and the light within you in an empowering way and you become your own self-destruction.

Sitting still for too long can also cause energy to stagnate inside your body and by its very nature, energy has to move. If you feel drained, exhausted or any other kind of negative emotion, moving your body can help to clear any energy that has started to build up inside of you. If energy is meant to move and you are made of energy, then you are meant to move too. As much as possible and at least once every other day.

This can be something as simple as standing up straighter and changing your posture, taking a tranquil walk in nature or something more intensive like going on a jog to loosen up those muscles and joints.

Foster new habits and ensure that this includes movement because this can help to create a happier, much more fulfilled you. Stimulate your mind, body and spirit in harmony with one another because all of them are equally important to the other.

What do I mean by spirit? By protecting your energy and being mindful of the energies that may have an effect on your mood and personality, you are looking after your spirit. When you stimulate your spirit, you put yourself around individuals that make you feel alive or people who bring out the best in you. You focus on your internal light, the Higher Power that spiritually guides you and act from a place of love.

Combine movement with activities that also stimulate your mind and spirit and you'll certainly start to notice a difference in your life.

A butterfly

When you think of a butterfly, what is the first word that comes to mind? For me, it represents transformation and I'm guessing that you too will have thought about a variation of that word. As you may know, butterflies evolve from a caterpillar, they were once in a different state, but they convert into a new form of life. It doesn't matter that the butterfly has only endured one stage of transformation, it has still gone through its very own transformative process.

I want you to think about this for a moment, and to see that you may also transform and improve your life, but unlike the butterfly who only has to do this once, for us it is an ongoing process. Throughout your lifetime, you are going to be given opportunities to transform and better who you are as a person. You must spread your wings and fly. You MUST continuously transform to reach a higher level of potential.

If you don't continuously develop, both professionally and personally, other people will, and they will overtake you in your particular field.

A blue butterfly is often considered as a sign of life and the blue ones are those that stand out the most *to me*. In most cultures, the blue butterfly is a symbol of acceptance, honour, and great energy. I urge you to harness the blue butterfly's energy in your life – become accepting, honour yourself and make fantastic choices. Decide to be a person that spreads positive, vibrant energy and shine the bright light that is inside of you.

Flowing water

Water is widely known to represent life, a newness of life. Approximately, 71% of the Earth's surface is covered in water and the oceans holds around 97% of the Earth's water. Water is all around us, in the air, in rivers and the lakes, in the icecaps and glaciers and even inside many forms of life (including us). Doesn't that show that water is important, and it is something we should appreciate? If you think of life and everything that surrounds us, the ocean (metaphorically), you and I are just a tiny drop in that ocean. We are tiny drops in the ocean of life. From dreams to intuition, magic and mystery, water holds endless inspiration. If you think about it, many of the deepest water sources are still unexplored, proving that water is still full of unlimited and untamed potential. Just like you and I, we are full of potential and are waiting to be explored. The universal undertone of water can remind us to stay grounded. Water flows with reason, rhythm and rhyme, and in doing so, it teaches us some important lessons.

> Water has a reason – it provides life, we have been provided with a life and it is for you to then discover what your reason for living is. Ground yourself by remembering your life purpose and aim to do so every single day. Focus on the reasons, focus on your why and this will help you to stay motivated and grounded, enabling you to reach your fullest potential.

<u>Water has rhythm</u> – it is consistently authentic. What I mean by this is that water never fails to disappoint, we know what it does and what it is there for. There is a sense of clarity when you think of water, it flows rhythmically. It flows in all sorts of directions, but it is consistent in nature, in force and in power. Harness water's rhythm in your life – use rhythm to your advantage by building up the momentum with positive, healthy habits in order to share the light inside of you with others.

<u>Water has rhyme</u> – it is so therapeutic that it becomes melodic in your heart and in your soul. When you hear the ocean-waves crash together or you hear the sound of the sea washing up the sand on the shore, a sense of calm can often be felt. It's our life blood, we rely on it to keep us going and we are designed to be around – and in – water. This continuous flow of movement has the potential to open up your mind to new possibilities and to new thoughts. You can channel your energy in such a way that you become at one with water. Share this rhythmic power that water has with other people and become a reliable positive flow of movement that people can feel and witness.

From a spiritual perspective, you can connect with water in a powerful way. The regularity of water across human cultures demonstrates the sacred value of life. Water connects life and brings humankind together because water is the supply of life.

Using water as guidance, you can be a permanent supply of life for the rest of the world, all by

The Light Within You

believing in yourself and utilising your incredible, infinite power.

Water symbolises purification, protection and healing too. When you relate to something bigger and more powerful than you are, you are putting yourself in the same category as that element. In doing so, you are opening up your mind to the possibility of becoming just as big and great as that – *'association breeds similarity.'*

As we discussed earlier, who you associate with often rubs off on you and helps to influence the person you become. Choose your influences wisely, place your trust and guidance in the sources and people that have the power to change your life. Surround yourself by those people and items that you want to become.

Curiosity is the key to life. Keep asking questions and open up the door to a whole world of possibility. – GS

Super Strong

Super strong – your own personal strength manifests great power in moving you forward and along the way, discover a sense of serenity and hope that touches others.

You are stronger than you know

I overheard a conversation on the train before and it was one that really got my mind ticking. '*It's so silly that I leave my work to last minute...*' and then they continued with their conversation. Is it me or is that one of life's most common problems and I bet that you've done it in the past, just like I have too? We do, as part of our human nature, tend to leave things to last minute.

The vast majority of people tend to procrastinate for so long and put off what is really important, occupying themselves in areas that have no positive impact on their life. Anything to avoid tackling the task at hand. And so, prioritising our agenda is necessary for all of us and knowing when there is the time and the place that permits for action. This has happened to me on many occasions too. I will be under pressure, knowing I have multiple different pieces of work to do, but I worry about starting. I don't know about you but starting is always the hardest part. Once you start, you tend to get yourself into a flow and that helps you to gain momentum. When you're trying to get something done, flow is the optimum state to be in and it's something that you should strive for whenever you can. Being in flow means that things run smoothly, that one tasks moves to the next and that everything happens with little to no resistance. But getting into flow, and indeed starting, can be the hardest part.

If you find yourself in this state it can be worth exploring exactly what it is that you are feeling and why you are so reluctant to start. Often there can be some underlying resistance to the task at hand, exploring it will help you to understand what is going on. Here are a few questions that can help:

What feeling do I feel towards this task (fear, dread, overwhelm, anxiety, perfectionism, etc)?
Am I afraid that something could go wrong?
What is the first, most basic step I can take to get this project moving? (If you are writing a book, like me, start by opening the document, naming it and writing the title.)

If I've learnt anything about the art of starting something that you want to do, it is to just to get started.

Don't fall into the trap of waiting for the motivation to come to you, because the motivation can just as easily follow action. Take that first step and you'll find yourself powering through the task and before long, it will all be done.

A new strategy that I recently learned and would like to share is that I set the date for when a particular task has to be completed by and I write this date in my diary and on my phone under notes. Once I have done this, I work backwards from that date by setting small milestone tasks and I schedule them within the time frame I have. Once I have broken the major task down into small, realistic and achievable steps, I am able to forget about the end result and solely focus on meeting my smaller targets. Doing this really helps me to break it down and I know that if I stick to my schedule, I will ultimately get the task done.

'You don't know how strong you are until being strong is your only option.'

We are all able to think and behave as if we are super strong, but it isn't until we find ourselves in situations that require such strength that we realise how strong we actually truly are.

Have you ever been around people who are going through a tough time and they depend on you for support? How did that make you feel? I'm guessing that you felt emotionally distressed for that person and it tore you apart on the inside. Did you crumble and break in two? Did you turn to them and say, *'I can't help you with that'* or *'this is too much for me, I can't cope'*? The likelihood is that you didn't, you stood up tall and you were there for that person because you wanted to support and comfort them. We all have compassion inside of us and the ability to empathise with others, it's what makes us human. Human connection is beautiful.

In those hard moments that could potentially damage and destroy us, we rise up with our greatest strength. If you can tell yourself that you have a light within you during those moments, you will inspire and move people in extraordinary ways.

It is not until we are faced with turmoil do we realise how incredibly strong we are. There is a profound strength inside each and every one of us, sometimes we just have to dig deep to find it.

Radiate strength

Positive energy is highly infectious and it's probably something that you have already experienced on numerous occasions. Have you ever been around somebody that cannot stop smiling, somebody who likes to share their humour with other people and somebody who just enjoys being kind and caring towards others?

Being positive can become another habit and you can easily get into a routine of thinking in a positive way. This is an incredibly powerful tool because by doing so you are making other people feel alive, making other people feel hopeful and you are lifting them up to a place centred on belief. What do I mean by that?

When I post on social media I have the intention of posting only positive, inspiring and uplifting material, the kind of material that I know will only feed and nurture the human soul. Of course, there are days when I'm feeling low, but I know that I don't need to promote or advertise that online. I have people that I can confide in on a personal level if I feel that I need to talk to somebody. Instead, I intentionally aim to write words of wisdom and share them with other people to try and make them *feel* something. Why? Because I know that everybody needs a touch of inspiration every now and then and I know that because I know how it makes me feel to read something empowering. Something that gives me that sense of belief. For example, somebody might be having a really bad day and they might need some hope to know that everything will be okay. Your post, your words, or an image you post may be just the thing that they need in order to feel better once again. By sharing your positive energy, whether that is on social media or through sharing it in real life, you are radiating strength. You are radiating light upon those around you. We have been gifted with a light as part of our human nature, as it allows us to *be* that strength, that spark of hope, that others may need when facing adversity. Have you ever looked around you and felt that you would like somebody to make you smile or that you would just like somebody to talk to? Everybody needs that strength once in a while and not everybody can find that strength when they most need it. Let's be there for each other.

In my family, we frequently say the words super strong to one another, to give that sense of hope during moments of hardship and challenge. The words *super strong* touches my heart when I hear them. They make me feel stronger on the inside and then as a result, everything on the outside feels like it will be okay.

If something in your life *is* or *feels* quite difficult at the moment, then just know that it's happening for a very good reason. Sometimes it's important that we are challenged in certain areas and accept that uncomfortable things may happen so that we can learn from the experiences and ultimately grow from them.

How could you possibly teach or give back and help other people if you have not gone through the thing that you are trying to teach? It is virtually impossible, and it is also unethical to advise or support somebody with something if you haven't gone through it yourself. Hold onto your integrity and make sure that you are a person of your word. What do I mean by that?

If you believe that you are capable of being strong for others, then you need to be in the right mindset yourself in order to give back in a positive way. You need to look after yourself first. You need to be using the strength from one of your life lessons and gain the strength from other areas of your life (from the input that goes inside your mind on a daily basis from what you consume, which could be from reading a book for example). You need to make a conscious effort by deciding to not let the external world affect you and your mind, because if you do, you are damaging your emotional state and the potential of what you can positively offer those around you.

You may not be able to be your best self at the moment and perhaps that's something that you need to work on, but don't give up. There are so many people out there that need you, whether that is your family, or it could be a friend, or it may be a stranger that is a friend you haven't met yet. Don't ever underestimate the power and positive effects that you can have on other people. You truly have a gift; you have a light within you that needs to be shared with others. Be the power force that you desire to see more of in the world, what you would like to feel from other people, because *'you are what you think you are.'*

Ignite hope

When one of life's challenges comes along it is easy to get so caught up that the feeling of hopelessness becomes a bigger problem than the challenge itself. It is easy to be stuck in a dark place and feel disheartened, disappointed and hopeless about your chances of coming out of it. You may think *'this is it, there is no way out'*. It can destroy your soul and if you let it, destroy your life.

Life is precious, and you shouldn't put yourself through such cruel pain because you deserve to feel a sense of peace. You deserve the best and to have and be whatever it is you want in life. Being hopeful means, you can think that the future will be better in comparison to the present moment and you are fuelled with an enriched belief that you have the power to make it through to the light. If we flip that over to being hopeless, that means that you would believe that the future cannot be any better, there are no improvements ahead because you don't think you have the power to move forward. But you do.

It truly is the leading indicator of success in so many areas of life: in your career, your private/personal business, in your studies and even in your relationships. Hope is exceptionally beneficial for our overall wellbeing. If you think about it carefully, when you are feeling hopeful about something, it doesn't really matter what life throws at you as you feel prepared and equipped with the mindset to accept the challenge and overcome it. Adopting a hopeful mentality can improve with time. The more you practice being hopeful, the more hopeful you will become.

When we think about the theory of *self-fulfilling prophecy* (everything that you believe in your mind, whether it is true or not, you result in believing to be true), if you believe that everything will be okay in a dark situation, you are convincing yourself that it *will* be the case. You are training your mind to believe that even if the outcome is bad, it won't destroy you because you will just simply learn a life lesson during those moments. *Every cloud has a silver lining.*

Holding on to faith means that you have a positive and active approach to life and you wish to nurture your internal spirit. The spirit radiating your light. Perhaps you want to appreciate and value life much more and you know that deep down inside of you, you need to spark that hope, that beautiful, burning fire that can keep you away from the darkness.

You can make an informed decision as to whether or not you choose to be hopeful about something because your hope lies in your attitude and in what you program your mind to think. Of course, we have autopilot thoughts that come into our minds all of the time, but we have to consciously push them out and focus on the thoughts that empower us to stay strong. You and I have to protect our souls from falling weak. We must hold on to our faith.

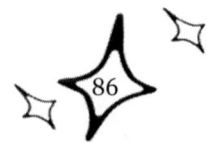

This won't be possible all of the time, even I know how enlightening it can feel to just have an *off day* and sob my heart out to its full content. We all need to have a little cry now and then, but that's absolutely okay. The power in those moments lie with acceptance – accepting the things you cannot change – and knowing that the moment shall pass, and you shall rise again.

When you are feeling upset, don't reject the emotion and get angry that you are feeling that way, learn to accept and sit in observation to the moment. Reflect upon your feelings and think about what it was that caused you to feel that way. You can then think about what you might decide to do differently next time and gain something valuable from the experience. There would be no real happiness or joy without pain and sadness... the dark times remind us how treasurable the fulfilled moments of light are, those moments that make you light up inside with pure joy and happiness. Rejoicing is a sacred experience, but we would probably not recognise its existence without the comparison of hardship in our lives. You have to remember to *stay strong* and *trust* in your emotions, your *inner guidance system*. Don't let those dark phases destroy you, instead be thankful for them and reflect positively on them. Be thankful that they have built up your strength. The darkness doesn't define you or refrain you from a more fulfilled, self-empowering future. Remember, the light is *within* you.

Peace and positivity

Who are you? What is it that makes you *you*? What are your values?

For me, the one area of life that I most care about, on a daily basis, is personal growth and self-development. I have recently come to believe that fuelling our mind with the right *input* is crucial, if not the most important action that we can take. It can be quite easy for happiness to become temporary in our lives because life happens and so much goes on around us all of the time. We process thousands of thoughts every single day, so we are constantly taking in new information, and sometimes that information isn't always positive or beneficial to our mind. This makes it even more important that we learn to top up our positive mindset.

We must make sure that we are making the right choices and choosing to consume content that is in our best interest and nourishing for our spirit. This could be listening to inspirational podcasts, watching empowering documentaries or praying to God. It could be reading encouraging self-development books such as this one. We need to find those enlightening stories so that we can *feel* good, even if it is for a short while. When we do, the effects on our mind, and on our personal progress, is exceptional.

For example, when I'm sitting at home and I can feel myself feeling a little flat, tired and overworked, I might decide to watch self-development experts Tony Robbins or Brendon Buchard. I think it takes approximately 5-10 minutes of watching and hearing one of them speak for me to feel *alive* again. It suddenly lifts me up to a higher state of happiness. I feel like anything is possible again. Now if I did that on a Monday and on Tuesday I didn't bother, because I didn't think it was necessary to do that two days in a row, I am fooling myself.

We have to make a purposeful effort to top up our positive mindset on a daily basis. Every single day we have to make sure we are intentionally enriching our minds. We are introducing ourselves to incredible content that makes us feel inspired, that makes us feel at one with ourselves again and limiting any content that doesn't. For me, living needs to be a continuous growth and development process and I intend to live as a lifelong learner.

Learn to *consciously* learn at every opportunity. If there is an upcoming seminar that you know you could really benefit from, attend it. If there is a networking event happening nearby and you know you could make some useful connections, go to it. Broaden your horizons and spread those wings of yours without any restriction. Allow yourself to connect with others and learn from them as they also learn from you. You owe that to yourself.

There is always *'sunshine after the rain'*. You've probably heard that saying a few times throughout your lifetime, and I am a true believer that we need to focus on strengthening our strengths instead of worrying about our weaknesses.

What are your *sunshine* areas? Which parts of you shine bright? Which fraction of your abilities can you really amplify and truly take advantage of?

For some reason, it often takes a dark exploration and a turmoil of emotions (the rain) to discover the bright solution (the sunshine). Again, we must think and remember the power of acceptance.

Learning to *accept* the rain and trust that the rays of sunshine are on the other side of it, no matter how overwhelming the rain might initially feel, can set you free on the inside. It can give you peace.

Practicing self-care is extremely important for you to become strong in this way. What is self-care? It means that you are actively being mindful of your own health and you are preserving it, keeping it in the best possible condition. You have a pro-active approach to protecting your wellbeing and happiness, especially when you might be sensing stress. You might have to give yourself some self-care by taking some days off work and recharging your batteries, or it could mean that you stop somewhere for a herbal tea and you just *be* for 15 minutes, looking out the window and watching the world go past. Perhaps for you, it's getting comfortable under a fluffy blanket and reading a book or taking a long soak with your favourite bubble bath. Or, it might be curating some content and ensuring that your input is fully in line with your best interests, your goals and values.

Put simply, self-care is making the most of whatever it is that makes you happy or allows you to feel joyful. Self-care is whatever you want it to be and whatever it is that charges your energy. You have to allow yourself time to rest, so that you can grow and be an even better version of yourself.

This also means that getting an excellent night's sleep is vital, as it allows your body to shut off for a while and to gain clarity for the next day. Before shutting down and going to sleep, remember to be thankful for the day you've had and if you can, write a gratitude journal. Try to find three things from the day that you can truly feel gratitude for and allow yourself to fully feel those feelings as you go to bed. Then, start to think about the following day and what you want to stem from it. What do you want to do, what do you want to achieve and how do you want to feel? Paint a picture of the ideal day in your mind and allow yourself to feel those feelings.

From my perspective, one thing I do every morning when I wake up is I tell myself *'no matter what life will throw at me I know that I can, and I will get through it'*. By reflecting and thinking in this way, you are allowing yourself to prepare for overcoming anything that life may throw at you. You are telling your inner voice that you deserve a fruitful day ahead. You are sending out all of the right signals. You are preparing for success.

Peace of mind means that you are happy with your own actions and that you are open and allowing yourself to be proud of your achievements. A lot of us probably fight and battle with our own minds on a daily basis and it can often hold us back in a bid to protect us. Unfortunately for us, our subconscious mind is still set to monkey mode, and this can often mean that it acts on misguided feelings of fear. It tricks us into being scared of something that can help us advance and it can sometimes be hard to get past this.

As a result, we can get stuck in our ways and not allow ourselves to perform to our truest potential. In doing so, we can often self-sabotage our own success, essentially ruining our chances before we've even started. Being and feeling peaceful in yourself is where true magic can happen.

Sometimes you have to make a conscious effort to step out of our *own way*, allow yourself to stride forward whilst knowing that you *are* worthy of success.

One thing that you can do to give yourself permission to step forward, is to practice accepting your past failures and mistakes, so that they cannot hold you back anymore. You might have heard the saying '*in order to love others, you must first learn to love yourself*'. Self-love doesn't just happen, and it certainly doesn't happen overnight, and for most of us it's something that we have to practice throughout our entire lives. In order to love yourself fully it takes much more than years of external influences. We must continuously look inwards and work on ourselves in a bid to self-improve, develop and grow into the person we want to remain or become.

There's a mistaken belief that if you want to better yourself and change your life, you have to feel a disconnect from who you are right now. But that is not the case. It is possible, even essential, for you be prepared to love yourself in the present moment, knowing that it means you can still want more.

By having peace in your heart and learning to accept you as you are – whilst knowing that you can still have more – you are telling yourself that whatever it is, it is all okay.

You are self-aware and consciously keeping yourself in the present moment, in the *here and now*, so that you can fully enjoy and embrace life right now. You are giving yourself compassion, love and reassurance without knowing it. This is why being self-aware is extremely important for us. If we want to have a clear mind and operate on an optimum performance, we need to gain clarity of self. Once we have worked out our strengths and our weaknesses, we can think of the solutions to the problems. We can evaluate and fix. We can have a *'growth mindset'*. Once you are aware of your dreams, hopes and wishes, you are able to take steps toward them. But you must make sure that you *act*.

Daily reflection can be exceptionally powerful in helping us to achieve internal peace while evaluating your own self, and that's why I suggest adopting a daily journal habit.

Journaling is worthwhile, as it allows you time to reflect on exactly where you are in your journey, simply through writing down your thoughts. Alternatively, you might prefer to express yourself artistically (whatever works best for you). Find a time that suits you best and allow your thoughts and feelings to spill onto the page in front of you. Just like a jug of water being emptied into a stream, your mind can only be clear if you act to help empty it. Once you've written your thoughts or feelings by writing them down, your mind will find it a lot easier to adjust to whatever it is that you have in front of you. Solutions or *next steps* should start to appear in the forefront of your mind.

To reach your goals and achieve profound peace, you need to not just have plans, but be mindful of optimising those plans along the way with thoughtful effort and action.

The Light Within You

You only know how strong you are when being strong is your only option... it becomes a painful struggle that develops into a power that can heal, transform and change lives. – GS

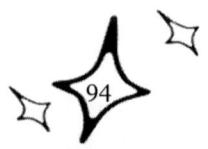

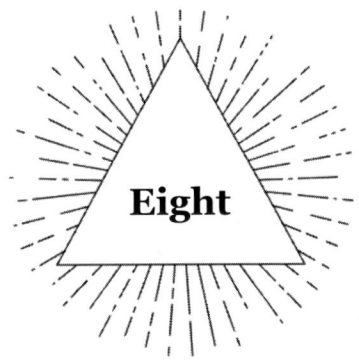

Sharing the Love

Share the love – underpin the true gems of love and understand ways of recognising it all around you. Love is the answer. Love breaks boundaries. Love stands for something bigger than our self.

Spontaneous acts of kindness

Love is a powerful word but how do you, personally, understand it? Do you think of relationships when you think of love? Most people do, but to me, love comes in many different forms. You can have love towards your pet, which is a different type of love that you would have towards a friend. You may love your job differently to the way you love your family or your partner. Love *is* beautiful and should be a celebrated part of your life. At every possible opportunity, adopt the mindset of *sharing* love because love does matter, and love can save the world.

A big part of love stems from giving because generosity is important for making connections with other people. You might have heard the saying '*you give to get*' but for me, that is not entirely true. The way I see it, you will manifest more by giving but sometimes, it's lovely to give and to not expect anything in return. If receiving is always your motive behind giving or doing, then it's probably the wrong reason to give. Ultimately, it's an unethical reason for giving. On the other hand, committing small, random acts of kindness every day, just because you want to, is achievable and highly rewarding.

For example, if you are at work and you know that you and your colleagues are working on the same thing and you finish before your colleague does, share your ideas and insight with that person. If you can, make that person's life easier, why not? Wouldn't you like someone to do that for you? Why should you want to keep your knowledge and know-how to yourself? Share the love. What happens is something truly magical, having been that generous in a pure-hearted, meaningful way, eventually the kindness that you shined upon that person will come back around. You might have inspired that person to do the same thing in return or it might come back to you in a more abstract less, obvious way. But somehow, when the time is right, that kindness will then be bestowed on you.

'You will receive abundance for your giving... the more you give, the more you will have.' – by W. Clement Stone. Isn't this a lovely quote? It truly resonates with me because giving generously is often a selfless act. A random act of kindness means that you are intentionally trying to assist somebody with something, who may be in a dark place, and as a result, you are likely to make other people smile and feel cared for and valued.

Sharing the Love

Yet sometimes, our insecurities and self-esteem can prevent us from being generous to other people and in turn, these qualities can stop us from receiving in turn too. Put simply, if you are feeling unworthy, then you believe that you have nothing valuable to give to others. And so, due to our own feelings of inadequacy, we can often feel questionable to people who then try to give to us. You may start to overlook the heartfelt, spontaneous gesture and instead begin to wonder why, often settling on a negative interpretation. Perhaps you draw conclusions from their gesture, assuming that they are being malicious or offending you in some way. Instead, if somebody does something kind for you, accept it joyfully and show gratitude. You deserve to be treated that way and perhaps that'll inspire you to do the same for somebody else. Let's be real for a moment, can you imagine a world where no one gave anything to each other? Where everybody just looked after their own needs but ignored everybody else's?

By now, you must have heard the saying that '*what goes around comes around*' and so give with all your heart, as much as you can, and always try to shine your light upon other people. We must treat others in the same way we would like to be treated.

Giving to other people can become a way of life and it can become an essential part of your own life's purpose. In return, you can benefit from the feeling that you gain from helping, supporting and offering yourself to others. Learn to use that receiving feeling to benefit your own life and support your own wellbeing.

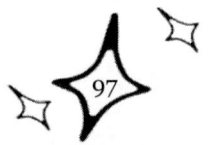

Through giving, you can become a person that has a purpose much bigger than your everyday life, much greater than what your current life priorities are worth. You may realise that the biggest feeling of satisfaction derives from giving back and being there for others. Only then, when you sacrifice yourself and adopt a selfless mindset, will you truly become a person that lives for a much greater purpose. This mindset of giving should stick with you and drive your daily journey forward, giving you a priceless sense of belonging, reason and purpose.

Offering someone a well-deserved compliment or feeding the homeless may make something that is worth chasing, something that is better than just feeling good. An act of sincere kindness can make you feel human.

Empathy

As we have just discovered, random acts of kindness are super important, and this can significantly impact our wellbeing. Giving and empathising with others can liberate us from our self-obsessions, selfishness and even help with feelings of isolation or loneliness. Deciding to adopt an open and loving nature can nurture your soul in so many ways and it's a sure-fire way to improve your pathway of being.

Empathise with other people, give without any expectation of a return and be there for someone because you genuinely care, and you are bound to see it pay-off in your own life. Showing that you are willing to put yourself in their situation and understand where they are coming from, can be a mutually beneficial experience. By being there for someone in that way, you are giving them the opportunity to free themselves from their troubles, anxiety or any deep-buried pain. As the old saying goes, *'a problem shared is a problem halved.'* Be the person that others turn to.

How would that make you feel if someone were to do that for you? I bet that it would make you feel on top of the world. Do you think that it would free and release you from those dark emotions? It most likely would.

Empathy was first introduced in 1909 by a psychologist called Edward B. Titchener and it literally means *feeling into*. Put simply, empathy means that you're able to understand what another person is experiencing and relate to them in an emotional way.

Everybody knows that the world can be a cruel place, one skim through a newspaper and you can see how much cruelty is occupying the world. From natural disasters to unnatural disasters and all the crimes that humans commit.

But why do people often avoid becoming a more self-serving, compassionate individual?

There is some evidence to suggest that there are neurobiological components that make up empathy. Our brain is incredibly wired and without the ability to empathise, you might never be able to fully understand experiences that are unknown to you (this can be the case for real or imaginary characters).

The Light Within You

Why is it important to empathise? Empathy allows people to build and strengthen their social connections with others. Being empathetic, you are able to respond appropriately to any given social situation. Taking empathy onboard also allows you to regulate your own internal emotions. In doing so, you are often able to reflect on your own life and learn to depict how you feel about something, without feeling overwhelmed. Despite some people being unable to empathise with other people, often due to personal reasons, most people are able to, in many, if not all situations.

It is remarkable to be able to view the world from the same perspective as somebody else and we should be grateful when expressing that quality. And it is one that we should choose to hone. Praise and celebrate empathy moments.

It is moving to realise that empathy has the potential to empower all of us and to give us the opportunity to help improve somebody else's suffering. Acknowledging this should enlighten each and every one of us and enable us to all utilise this underestimated strength to make the world a better place.

Being in touch with your own emotions means that you are able to self-assess and analyse your internal voice, allowing it to respond in the most positive manner possible. There is no point in us ignoring our inner voice, after all, we all have a light within us and it's important that we learn to trust it.

Love in all areas

How far are you willing to go to become the best version of yourself? Is there ever an end point? For me, the answer to this question is really simple and, in my mind, there should never be an end to self-development and it is something that we should embark on improving continuously. After all, self-development is food for our soul and it's just as important that we feed that area of our being as it is that we feed our bodies.

One aspect of self-development that can be transformational is that of *love* and how it can be used to heal others.

Sharing love with somebody else has the capacity to spark a vision of hope within them, and you, and in doing so you are warming up their heart and their soul and making them feel loved.

When you share love, you are showing them that you care, no matter what you are there for them and you may just be the light that a person needs to guide them out of a dark time. It could be you that does that for somebody else, just by radiating your love or it could be that they are able to do that for you. After all, love has the power to heal and mend broken souls.

Everybody wants to feel loved at some point in their life, even if they don't admit it or are not aware that they want it. I have found that the more love I give, the more love I receive. Just as kindness can often bring back more kindness, the same standard applies for love. If you give love selflessly and

radiate love in all that you do, love will reverberate to you.

People can always feel the warm energy that comes from a place of love and we should all strive to mirror that in every loving act. No matter how great the results I achieve in the other areas of my life are, without feeling loved and getting treated with respect and kindness, there will always be something missing. It will feel like there is a gap, an empty space, as though something needs to be filled. When you feel unhappy and unsatisfied, try to make someone else happy. Their happiness is likely to unleash happiness in you as well. Like attracts like and what you give, you tend to always get back.

Love has power because love connects and transcends positive emotions and energies between souls. Love *is the answer* to most turmoil moments of adversity and it breaks through boundaries. I believe that if the world focused on love, gave love and received it with open arms, there wouldn't be so many problems in the world. *'Love is the solution to all problems and the medicine to all that there is.'*

Yet it can often be hard to be vulnerable, difficult to open up and frightening to give your world to another person. It's difficult and sometimes, for some people, trust has to be earned. But one of the problems I think most of us experience is knowing and learning to let go of the past. *'Love freely, let go of the past, live for today and feel free on the inside.'*

Sharing the Love

Love is special, and although some of us may believe that it cannot be physically seen, touched or heard, we all know that it can truly be felt within the heart. Treasuring those that you love should be a life priority, life is precious, and you never know when you are going to need the ones you love. It's something we shouldn't take for granted, as none of us know what tomorrow will bring. I LOVE love. Can you say the same?

Unity, community, you and me

Being a part of something bigger than yourself (me, myself and I) gives you a sense of purpose, a sense of direction and it can help give you a place to belong. Feeling in unity with other human beings can spark a buzz inside and that can become quite addictive. When I was training to be a teacher, I used to really look forward to my training days where I could socially catch up with like-minded individuals who inspired me and made me feel excited about life. Being around people that were travelling down the same path as me, helped to make me feel alive and it gave me strength to see the journey through. When I felt like giving up, they gave me hope, especially during the difficult times of becoming a teacher.

Being a part of something bigger than myself allowed me to gain perspective on my situation as a trainee teacher and I always knew that other people were experiencing it too. It is said that who you associative with is important to who you become, as quite often, you are shaped by the personalities and the habits of the people around you. But you know that you are in the right room, with the right people, when they inspire you or when you feel that they are shining their light on you. That's where the true power in being a part of something can be seen. Go for it and have those, what may feel like, awkward conversations with strangers who may eventually become some of your truest friends.

I believe that in order to be in unity with other people and part of something bigger, a community, you have to be and feel proud of who you are. When you are able to truly be yourself and be the most authentic true version of you that you can possibly be, you will find that it is much easier to fit in.

Throughout my life I have realised that when I use things that I personally like, I often perform better. For example, when I was at college, I decided to use princess and Minnie Mouse notepads to write my notes in because I have always liked cute things, especially princess-themed things. I thought that if I used those notepads, they would make me feel happier when I was working. And I was right. Likewise, with minions because I absolutely love them. So, what do I do? I use a minion flask for my tea. It may sound ridiculous, but I can reassure you that for me, being proud of who I am and not being afraid of showcasing my personality and my guilty pleasures, I am a much happier, fulfilled me. The same idea applies with colours too. If there is a particular colour that you like, why not introduce some of it around you? For example, I like the colour pink, so my phone case is sparkly pink, my laptop is pink, and my refillable water bottle is baby pink. Just feeling and experiencing my favourite colour in my daily life comforts me in a way that helps me to achieve a sense of self-love and appreciation for my true identity. In doing that, I

am allowing the true me to shine through and this helps me to further connect with other people.

Are we selfish when we are putting ourselves first? Being selfish is to be selfless because by giving yourself what you need in order to become the best type of *you* possible, you are helping to make the world a better place. The more people who are authentically and entirely themselves, the better the world becomes. The more people who choose to share their light, unapologetically, the brighter each light will shine.

Every failure should be viewed as a win because you are in a position to learn and grow into a better *you*. It's not always about the end results and sometimes our biggest failures contain our biggest lessons and they are wins in the long-term vision for our lives.

A lot of people have their own perspectives on particular words, but universal law determines that we can each create our own view. Words can relate to us in different ways and the word selfish is open to interpretation. So, is being selfish really as bad as many may presume? Is there not power in self-development, in putting yourself first on some occasions in order to thrive? I would say that there is because by bettering ourselves, we are helping the wider community of the world.

When we fuel our minds and find our internal drive, we have a duty to respond to that. Somebody who is self-assured, clear about their goals and speaks up for themselves may appear as *selfish* but on the other hand, he or she may just be very equipped to become successful. When you see the success of others, instead of seeing them as selfish, feel gratitude and now that what is possible for them is also possible for you.

What happens when you become successful and abundant in areas of life that matter to you? You put yourself into a powerful place where you have the ability to be able to transform lives and help others. Once your cup is full to the brim with life, with personal success, with joy and with the ability to share abundantly, you can then begin to overflow, then you can truly enrich the lives of others.

At this point, you can then share that light within you, the light deep inside of you, with others. Being selfless opens you up to other people, giving you the potential to share your light with others. Choosing to be selfless opens the heart and mind to the rest of the world, removing the tunnel vision that selfishness can offer. Selfishness and selflessness encompass one another, they are in a magical cycle and each is the other's co-factor. Both are needed, and both support one another. If you didn't know selfish, you couldn't know selfless and so both have a part to play. One is not possible without the balancing of the other.

Without the ability to look after yourself and your needs, you are risking damage to the most important person of all, the person that can achieve greatness in life – you. It is during those moments that we are fully aware, responsible and give ourselves permission to selfishly love ourselves and selflessly love others. And during those moments we become even more in touch with humanity, ourselves and who we really are as people.

Sharing the Love

Keep smiling and watch the world smile with you. I can almost guarantee you, it will make you feel complete on the inside and out when you share your warm-gifted energy, even if it is for a slight moment. – GS

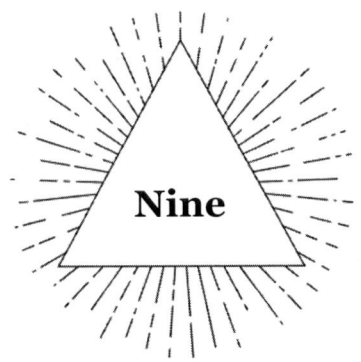

Reborn

Reborn – comprehend the power of manifestation and understand how praising, as an act, can take you to incredible places of joy, happiness and serenity.

Ask, act, believe and receive

How often do you ask for what you want? Have you ever sat and wrote down, specifically, everything that you want to achieve in your life? If you have, that's excellent and you are already one step ahead but if you haven't, it's something worth doing.

There is a real importance in being clear on what you want, not vaguely or abstractedly but specifically knowing exactly what it is that you want. If you're not clear, how do you know what actions need to be done in order to achieve the desired outcome or what vibration you need to be on?

I'm sure that you have heard of the saying that *'like attracts like'* but have you ever heard of the Law of Attraction? In essence, the law of attraction is focused on asking for what you want, and once you have asked and followed it through, it is given to you by a Higher Power. For me, I regularly ask for what I want through prayer. William Walker Atkinson used the phrase Thought Vibration or the Law of Attraction in the Thought World, 1906. But the New Thought understanding of the world originates from the teachings of Phineas Quimby in the early 19th century. During the early stages of his life, Quimby was diagnosed with tuberculosis and despite there being no reliable cure during this period, Quimby noticed that moments of excitement were relieving him from his pain. Quimby then committed to studying the idea of *Mind over Body* and made it his mission to understand how influential taking advantage of this power can be for any human being.

Let's dive into the concept a little more. The idea behind the Law of Attraction is that what you think about you bring about and that you attract based on your energy in the present moment, the here and the now. Your energy is determined by your collection of thoughts, feelings and beliefs and so in order to manifest something specific, you have to ensure that you are on the same vibration, or in the same energy as that which you wish to attract. Your energy determines your vibration, so both terms are one and the same.

This means that you have to truly believe and feel that you can have anything you want, and it can be beneficial to intensely think as if you already have it. Once you realise that there is a higher, infinite power and that you have a *light within you*, you can deliberately direct your attention towards the things you want. Where your attention goes, your energy flows and that helps you to manifest your dreams and lifelong goals. All whilst having faith and knowing that your reality should naturally manifest for you (with the right attitude, positive mind-set and actions to follow).

In order to utilise this law and to use it for your advantage, it's important that you practice the mindset tools and management concepts that we talked about in earlier chapters. Because our minds often try and play tricks on us, creating resistance, self-sabotage or doubt, this can prevent us from aligning with our goals. So, it is important that you are cautious. Your mind may try and distract you from your success or try to make you procrastinate on the actions that are needed to manifest what you desire. That's why it is important that you ask clearly for what you want, in any way that works best for you, and believe that it is entirely possible and act upon achieving it. In doing so, you will then receive what you truly deserve as a result. In the same way, answers will manifest from your prayers. Of course, none of this would be possible without faith and trust in the Higher Power, a force who is there to guide you and provide you with the strength that you may not be able to find yourself. For me, this is God.

Do you know that you are worthy of so much in this world? Strive to generate those feelings of already having what you want, right now. It doesn't matter that it may only be experienced for a few minutes here and there, it's not the time that counts, it's the intensity of the feeling. The more passionately you feel about what it is that you want, even if it is just for a second, the higher your chance of success in achieving it is likely to be.

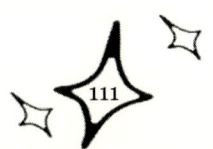

When I was doing my teacher training, I was introduced to the concept of the '*golden moment*'. For the golden moment you sit and focus on everything that you are grateful for, you put yourself in a place that you desire, and imagine that you have everything you could ever want or need. This, for me, was an incredible breakthrough as it was something I had never experienced before. It is a powerful visualisation strategy that really worked for me and I admired the concept of it being a *golden* moment.

You can call this process of visualisation whatever you want, whatever it is that resonates with you personally. You may have already heard of the saying that you have to '*fake it until you make it*' and this idea can be perfectly applied to the law of attraction. Essentially, manifestation experts believe that if you *act as if* the goal is already yours, you heighten your chances of having it. After all, that is another powerful way of stepping into the feelings, the energy and the vibration of that which you are seeking to bring into your reality.

You don't need to know how you are going to do something, that is the Higher Power's job, you just have to know that you will. The way will be shown to you when you are ready to see it. When you ooze with faith, trust and believe that you can, and you will receive your manifestation, the world will feel lighter, the weight lifts, the darkness fades and in that place the light should appear.

Another powerful law of attraction tool that can be used to help you generate a consistent and constant flow of positive traction, is to create your very own vision board. I made my first one when I was at university. I printed out pictures of everything I wanted to have in the future, cut them out and pinned them onto a board. I would then leave my vision board in front of my bed so that every morning when I woke up and every night when I was going to sleep, I would see those images and focus on what it was that I wanted. Don't just concentrate on the *what* of what it is that you are trying to manifest; remember the importance of focusing on the *feelings*.

For me, when I started to use these practices, it was weird because out of nowhere I would have a realisation about how I could achieve something on my vision board. This is regarded to be *inspired action* because once you have asked and made it your intention to manifest something, the Higher Power will often send ideas into your consciousness. These ideas might be just what you have needed to push you over the edge into receiving your manifestation or it might be one more step that will get you closer to your goal. It doesn't matter, just know that you have been given this idea for a reason and it should there to be acted on, in faith. Where possible, always follow the ideas the moment that you are able to do so and don't sit on them for too long.

Sometimes, the more we focus on something, the easier finding the answers and the *way* becomes.

We must give ourselves time to think, space to breathe and provide ourselves with an allowance to forget about everybody else for one moment, in order to focus on our internal truths and manifest what truly matters to us. *To you.*

You reap what you sow

There is real truth in the quote '*you reap what you sow*' and it's exactly what underpins the laws of the universe. Put simply, whatever energy you put out into the world, you are likely to receive the exact same energy in return. In an earlier chapter we talked about the idea of random acts of kindness and how such acts can then inspire another, and perhaps that was the perfect example. The more kindness that you put into the world, the more kindness you will get back. Energy is vibrational and cyclical, it ebbs, and it flows but it also operates in harmony with other people because like attracts like. A thought moves from synapse to synapse (a junction between two nerve cells) in the neurons of our mind and in doing so, it creates a chain reaction.

A single thought has the ability to fire through a series of controlled, pre-defined circuits that each provoke an emotional response, which in turn gives us a result. Each of our emotions has the ability to inspire a related action or behaviour. For example, a thought about love might lead to you kissing your partner. A thought about pain might lead you to crying. An angry thought might lead you to feeling resentment, depression or it may lead to you lashing out. This process doesn't just cause a response from within you, but it also attracts that same kind of energy. If you dwell in feelings of frustration, you will attract more people and circumstances to feel frustrated about but if you dwell in gratitude, you'll attract more to be grateful for.

You've probably noticed that when you are feeling happy, you attract happiness in the people all around you. You may have been feeling frustrated due to something happening at work and the next thing, you notice somebody else taking out their frustration on you.

It's for that reason that starting as you mean to go on is so important and having a positive, high-vibrational morning routine can change the entire outcome of your day. Ensure that your morning is full of reassuring affirmations and feelings of peace within yourself (by reminding yourself to stay present in the current moment). Find a successful morning routine that works for you. Put yourself in a mindset of success and emotionally feel into it throughout your day. Thoughts are things, they vibrate too, and what you think in your mind, you become in a version of your own reality.

It can be hard to stay on a positive track when perceived failures arise, and it is okay to sometimes feel like you have failed. But it's important to remember that it's not really a complete failure unless you chose to give up.

Sometimes, it takes for you to fail, several times, before you are able to succeed because you have a lot to learn about yourself and about the process first. You may need to equip yourself with the relevant skills and mindset and to build strength from the inside out. When you reach the point that you can accept perceived failure or mistakes, it will only serve to humble you. Manifestation expert and spiritual teacher, Gabriella Bernstein chooses to see mistakes and failures as detours that lead you in the right direction. Ultimately, a failure is only what you perceive it to be and it is you that attributes any meaning to it. Instead of choosing to interpret it as a judgement on you, your worthiness or ability to go after your goal, choose to see it as a detour or a lesson. Decide what you can take away from this attempt and get back on top.

For example, being a teacher there are many instances when things don't quite go the way I want it to and it can throw me off, put me into a bad mood and make me feel emotionally stressed. If I decide to allow that to have an effect on me and control my mood, I would take my emotions out on my children and that wouldn't be fair. It's important for me to stay in control of my emotions and to take charge in adopting the right mindset because after all, I am the children's role model. I need to model the right attitude and behaviour that I expect from them (like a mirror reflection). You get back what you put into the world because everything is connected, and it all vibrates through the oneness that binds all of us together.

Complain and remain or praise and be raised

If you feel that you are easily affected by negative behaviour, then shift your focus. Don't concentrate on the negative situations around you. Don't focus on the negative individuals that want to speak meanly about others. Why would you want to be a part of that? That doesn't mean that you necessarily have to stay away from such people, but you have to learn to find inner peace in those situations and take the viewpoint of a learner. Learn from these experiences. If you want to feel good, send out the right signals and then witness extraordinary things unfold in your life. Feeling angry or resentment towards someone or something? Release that negative energy. Unlock those negative blocks and let go. Forgive people for their wrongdoings because you are only hurting yourself by holding on to resentment. It is *you* that is suffering from it, not them. Only through forgiveness can you move forward and feel serenity in your heart. This also applies to yourself too, so learn to forgive others and also yourself.

The saying '*when you complain you remain, praise and be raised*' by Joyce Meyer truly resonated with me when I first heard it. The more that you complain about something, the longer you will stay in the same situation because by universal law you are attracting even more to complain about. You are creating and reaffirming the negative energy to yourself, reminding yourself about all the badness in a particular situation and in doing so, asking for more of the same. I bet when you complain about something you don't feel one glimmer of hope or positivity? You feel darkness, like there is no light inside of you, or around you, because it is not what you are attracting to you. Where energy and focus go, manifestation flows and so the more and more you focus on a lack of something, more of that thing you will see.

When you complain, you are choosing to keep yourself in the same situation. On the other hand, when you praise other people and show optimism about something you might not necessarily agree with, you are shining light on what could be a bad situation. Choose to show hope, gratitude and willingness to learn in any negative situation and you'll quickly flip your feelings into the positive energy that we should strive for. Always look for the gratitude in any situation and learn to start seeing things from new perspectives.

In doing so, you are offering hope when hope seems lost, allowing you to manifest even more hope inspired situations. Focusing on contribution is one way to raise yourself to a higher state and learn to praise the fact that you can offer value. When you choose to focus on other people, you may realise that a current bad situation is not as bad as it seems. You may learn to appreciate the little things that you couldn't previously see, such as how fortunate you are to have a roof over your head or to have food in your fridge. When you praise the strong efforts that you do, you are showing self-love and are, in essence, *raising* yourself to a better place.

A place that can help you to share your *internal light* with others.

Do you have something in your life that is draining you, draining the life out of you? Cleanse yourself through acceptance and self-love because you deserve to be happy. If you are feeling negatively, that's an indicator to you that there needs to be a *change*. Don't wait for a change that you know is possible to happen, take ownership and work towards the desired result. It could be that you just want to feel lighter and all-round happier in your everyday life. Whatever it is that you want, you can decide to change it in an instant. In a single moment, you can make a choice to change the quality of your life by ridding the negative energy that lives within you. Accept the darkness by

remembering that your light shall prevail and then, keep rising to new heights.

Manifestation

'There is only one corner of the universe you can be certain of improving, and that's your own self.' – Aldous Huxley.

It is important to consistently and continuously ask yourself whether the goals you set align with your true self and with your identity. For example, you might set a goal to complete a course that you currently dislike and feel within you that something just *doesn't feel right*. It may be that at one point in time the course was indeed right for you but now, with growth and new focus, you can see that it no longer fits with your life vision.

Of course, be resilient and give it a go for a while to make sure you are absolutely certain, but don't continue with something if you intuitively know that it is making you unhappy.

How can you manifest your true potential and harness that incredible power of yours if you're on the wrong track? It's actually pretty simple, you have to learn to bounce back from bad choices, ensuring that you reflect on them and understand where it is that you went wrong in the first place. Once you've understood why you made that choice, you can then fix them and ensure that you make the right choices next time.

All too often we set goals and try to achieve them, despite the fact that they may not mean that much to us anymore. Why does this happen? We are human beings that are constantly changing and developing. And so, it is important to regularly take some time to analyse yourself and think about the things you are after. You must focus on what you want for it to manifest and take the right action through achieving one milestone at a time. At first, when you first set out on a path of enlightenment, it's worth setting aside some time each week to audit and correct your goals. Sitting down each week and asking yourself what your current priorities, feelings and choices are can then save you a lot of time in the long run. The earlier you learn about a change in your preferences, the sooner you can correct it moving forward. But remember, to just keep one foot in front of the other. Keep it simple and keep moving forward.

Ok, so what if you are not too sure of what you truly desire? What if you are having confused thoughts or questioning everything? What if you can't help but ask *why*?

As hard as it might be, try not to question too much because there is usually some unseen reason why you have been directed down a certain path. The Higher Power has guided you there. Often, you may be confused by the outcome of something, but it may be because you originally sent out the wrong signal. You made the wrong choice. In that case, you may have unknowingly asked for something that you didn't actually want.

To help prevent this from happening, it can be beneficial to start tracing your thoughts as this can allow you to either develop them into something (so that your desire becomes a truth) or to learn from

them and change them moving forward (remembering to find a worthy lesson).

It can be hard to have complete faith and belief in something that you cannot always see, but it's important to remember that there are many things that we enjoy in our life that we cannot see. Think about electricity and gravity. We cannot see the electricity travelling to turn on a light, but we know that it's there and it's working. Similarly, we know that gravity is working when something falls to the ground, but we cannot see the process happening. So, ask yourself, do you always need to see something to believe in it? Can *faith* be enough? To me, faith is one of the most essential parts of my being and it is what makes me who I am today. So yes, *faith* can and should be enough.

As much as possible, do not doubt that your manifestations will happen, have conviction so that you don't send out the wrong signal as that is one of the ways to prevent your dreams from becoming a reality. When you look inwards and examine yourself, ensure that you are being intentional and wholesome in your approach. Look at your dominant qualities, are they: compassion, respect, kindness, joy, patience, understanding and tolerance? Or are they on the other side of the spectrum: jealousy, resentment, anger and frustration? Magnify what you want by becoming the very best version of yourself.

Act upon opportunities that come your way and set positive intentions so that manifestations *can* and *will* take place. This is your life; this is your time... you deserve to have it all.

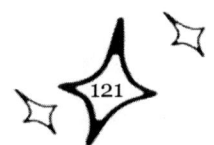

The Light Within You

As long as you treat people the way you would like to be treated in return, you are sending out the signals that invite compassion, kindness and entirety of being. – GS

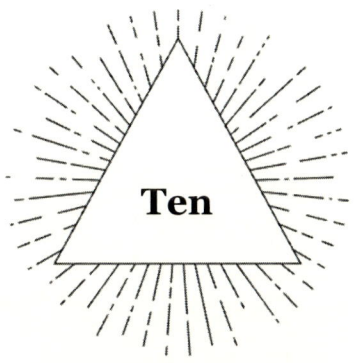

Plant the Seed

Plant the seed – the words inside this chapter transcend significant messages about unity, oneness, appreciation and staying conscious.

We are all connected

Where do your roots lie? Have you thought about your personal vine and how you interlink with others? Connecting with other people is proven, by counselling and therapy-based research, to be beneficial for our moods, and even for our overall wellbeing. Why is connecting with other people so important? Why is it vital that we continue to grow our relationship vine and spread our wings in this area? We all have a basic need to belong and it is one of our survival needs. From a very young age, we desperately try to connect and build relationships with people we believe to be trustworthy, as we understand that this helps us to grow and prosper into a thriving adult. Real connection is about much more than just talking to other people or sharing interests. If you think about it, sometimes when you have a conversation with somebody, you can talk to them for hours and not feel connected to them at all. In those moments, it

The Light Within You

can feel like an empty conversation with little worth or value attached to it. It's almost intuitive when we connect with somebody, it's something that you just feel and it's often very hard to explain. When you connect with another person there is a sense of being open, vulnerable, compassionate, empathetic and available to them, in the present moment.

It's worth therefore considering some psychological reasons why you might be finding it hard to connect with other people around you:

> <u>You feel alienated or different to other people, as though you see the world differently</u> but it's worth remembering that you are not alone, you are unique and that is a beautiful thing, something to be proud of.

> <u>You feel socially anxious when you interact with other people, especially people you don't know</u>. Try not to be afraid of people you don't know because a few short conversations later it might feel as if you have known them forever. Just remember that we are all connected, we are all as one.

> <u>In the past, people have said things to you like '*you're being difficult*' and now these comments have stuck</u>. But don't let other people's opinions define you, remember, what you think to be true will become true for you whether it's true or false. Take control of the image that you present to the world and choose to no longer be that person.

> <u>You have low self-esteem and don't value yourself very much</u>. In these moments, choose

Plant the Seed

to know your worth and remember that you have a lot to offer the world, there is only *one you.*

<u>You have trust issues that derive from your childhood</u>. As hard as it might be, learn to reflect on your childhood in a positive way because everything has happened for a reason. Everything has conspired to shape you into the person you are today and the challenges you experienced may have been needed to make you stronger.

<u>Previously you have found it hard to attach yourself to other people and have past trauma that lingers in your mind</u>. When you feel this way, be thankful for everything that you have gone through because without it, you may not have been able to become so powerful and inspiring to others going through a similar situation.

<u>You have suffered with anxiety before</u> but remember, it's good to talk to somebody about how you feel. Decide to open up and free yourself from dark, self-destructive thoughts, remember that you are *not alone.*

How might you connect with more people and plant the seeds to unite with them in a spiritual way?

> You could help somebody out of unconditional goodwill.
> Take the time to listen to somebody and take the opportunity to empathise with their situation.

> Have a personal conversation on a deep level with someone, where you truly open up and show vulnerability.
>
> Demonstrate gratitude towards another person, even if it is about a small thing such as just being a good listener or a good friend.
>
> Make eye-contact with a stranger or offer a genuine smile to somebody that you don't know.
>
> Share a beautiful experience with somebody.

You might be trying to grow your vine and plant the seeds of connection with other people and to do that you show that you are joyful, happy and willing to have a laugh. But be weary because it is possible to hide behind humour and in doing so, to not display your true, genuine self. If you find yourself doing this, it's likely that other people will start to notice and feel it too because of the spirit within us. Watch your ego. You must be able to be your complete self and trust the other person, or at least willing to show somebody that you consider them to be trustworthy. Work on yourself, every single day, and be conscious about your input. Your past doesn't define you and your future is yours to determine. What matters is how you take control *now*, how willing you are to realise you have a light inside of you and that people need to feel the unique power you possess; there is only *one* you.

How will you know if you have connected with somebody and you are on the way to growing your *vine?* You will feel the connection with them in that present moment. You will not be thinking or worrying about anything else, you will just be focusing on your shared interaction and experience with that person. You will feel that you are being completely yourself and that you have no reason to hold anything back. You will feel open, whether you are going through a sad time or a happy time, and it will liberate you internally. You will feel a genuine sense of empathy and kindness for somebody. You will lose focus on being judgemental and critical while embracing imperfection in a really beautiful way. You will feel that you can trust that person (which has probably happened without you realising it, just by allowing a stranger to help you with something, you are showing trust).

Open your eyes

When I say '*open your eyes*', I don't mean it in a literal way, but that you are aware of what is distracting you or of what is having a negative effect on you in some way. It is important that you reflect on this on a consistent basis, so that you can steer clear from being distracted. There is a time and a place to distract yourself and there is a time and a place for being present and focused at the task at hand.

For example, when you have decided that you need some shut off time, you can be willing and content with doing whatever it is you want (even if that means watching a Netflix series for three hours). In those moments, you must be able to be accepting of your need to rest and choose to not feel guilty for them. But also realise that if you do that too often, you are probably procrastinating from doing something much more significant, something much more purposeful and impactful for your future. It's about finding a balance and listening to your inner guide, knowing when you are procrastinating because of fear or when you just need to take a break. Being specific about who you are and what is your purpose will help you to take control of this part of yourself and to prioritise what is most important in the *here* and *now*.

Undoubtedly, technology has transcended our lives and opened us up to a whole new world. It has helped us to facilitate things in our life, everything has become that little bit more reachable, more possible, and all because of the internet. But we must be careful to not become a slave to what we have created. Planting the right seeds in your mind and developing a healthy mindset means that you need to be aware of everything that might be impacting you.

Why is being focused so important? When you are truly focused, you are able to take control over how you use your time and in doing so, you are able to make the right choices. Finding a balance between doing something meaningful, something that matters to you and knowing when to take a step back. By being this way, you are indirectly strengthening your soul and your ability to respond to any perplexing situation.

We cannot blame technology, but we can blame ourselves for how we choose to respond to the distractions that are around us. How can you sharpen your focus? If you can learn to harness your willpower and make the right choices, unconditionally, then you will be able to overcome damaging obstacles. Just like perceptions and our actions, our level of willpower is also under our control. Just like our muscles, with frequent personal development your willpower can improve. You may feel drained and exhausted after a hard day's work because you've had to make so many choices but be grateful for your mind's incredible abilities. You are capable of greatness.

Oneness

How can you take more control over your willpower and stay focused, for yourself? How can you start putting yourself first? This is a skill that I have worked on over the past few years and these are a few things that have helped me to move my willpower forward:

> Don't wait for the right time to act. The longer you put things off, the worse you're going to feel and ultimately, it's only you that you're hurting by not putting yourself first.

> Turn off your technological notifications and shut off from the world every now and then. Instead of using down time to have a social media binge, use that time to truly self-care, to take some time restoring your internal batteries and to just be alone with yourself.

> Switch off from everything that may be distracting you, that means forgetting about doing, and just *be*.

> Prioritise what the most important things to achieve are, for you at any one time, and focus on them only.

Use a countdown to bring yourself back into the present moment. Ask yourself, '*am I present right now?*' If not, what can you do to bring yourself back there.

Try exercising. Motion creates emotion inside of you so don't be afraid to change up your movement and release some of your built-up energy.

It is only once you have put yourself first, focused on *oneness* with yourself and what it is you need right now, that you can then focus on creating that same oneness with others. Sometimes, it can just feel like the missing pieces of the puzzle are revealed. You feel that two become one in an all-rounded way. You collaborate with people and share a mutual interest with them and then you feel that you are becoming as one with that person. There is no longer *you* and *I* but there is an *us*, two individuals coming together in unity. It's really important that you appreciate those special relationships where you just connect with someone else. Feel proud of joining together with someone else in a way that may not be able to be seen but touched with the heart. If you are looking to form those sorts of connections, make sure that you truly give yourself to somebody, open up and don't feel afraid to be vulnerable. There is true magic in real human connection and wonderful things may derive from it...

Appreciate and acknowledge nature

How often do you stop and look all around you? How often do you acknowledge and show awareness towards nature and all the incredible beauty outdoors? As far as I can remember, I have always enjoyed taking a slow stroll in nature, and for me, it has always been important. It refreshes my mind and allows me to think clearly again, especially when I'm feeling a little clogged up internally or I feel as though external forces in my life are draining the light energy out of me. I enjoy working outdoors, taking my book and reading at my local park (Raphael Park) while watching the big water fountain splash into the glistening lake. I absolutely love feeding the ducks, I find it therapeutic and, in those activities, I am entirely *present*. But how do these times profoundly impact on your life and the way you view it?

<u>Nature reminds us that we are not all that there is</u>. As much as we have an infinite power, it is important that you realise there is a much bigger life cycle around us where plants and animals live and die, making way for the next generation of life. Spending time in nature can remind us that even our own life operates on a cycle and we must take immediate action to find and embody our life art, which can then be amplified greatly through our internal light that we all have.

<u>There is no society influence when you are outdoors.</u> When you open the doors to nature it's as though you can lose track of time and space, allowing you to recharge and be present in that very moment. It can be a wholly spiritual activity, refreshing your soul just by stepping outside and removing anything man-made.

<u>Nature has a natural calming effect on the mind.</u> You can really gain perspective and see

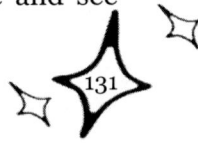

how small you are in the grand scheme of life when you are in the midst of the world outside. You will realise that nothing is permanent, things are constantly changing and evolving, and this should be taken as reassurance and peace of mind that nothing is ever for certain. You are consistently developing into the person you need to be. Make the most out of nature's stunning views, appreciate those sunsets and the picturesque sights of the water, mountain ranges or whatever it is you adore. Some of your best thoughts may derive from when you are spending time in nature.

The outdoors reminds us about the importance of living in harmony with one another. Hundreds of species (plants and animals) live among one another in the same environment. Try adapting that same mindset, each fragment of life contributes to a greater balance. We coexist together, in oneness.

Nature reminds us that there is always more to know and learn beneath the surface. If you think about it, when you witness a beautiful view of a mountain range or you watch the ocean washing the sand onto the shore, beneath the surface there are species being affected by climate change, by pollution and even through the action of nature's mighty force. You never know what sort of hardship a person is going through, even if they seem to be smiling on the outside. Always be mindful of the parts to people's lives that you may not necessarily be able to see.

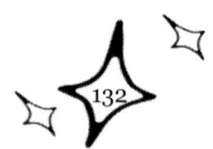

Plant the Seed

<u>The outdoors is a reminder that chaos and turmoil is a part of life.</u> Think about a thunderstorm for example. We can all enjoy a peaceful, beautiful sunny day, but what about those days that are cold, wet and fierce? Chaos is an inevitable part of life and you can choose to just accept that. Remember though, there will always be sunshine after the rain, just as long as you adopt the right mindset that will allow you to shine your light.

<u>Education is never-ending.</u> Just when you think you might know it all, you will learn something new because you will never know everything. We are not meant to know everything that there is to know because we are constantly learning. Humble yourself with the idea that you are consistently evolving, just like nature. There is always more to learn and an abundance to discover in the magical beauty that surrounds us, waiting for us to explore and reap the benefits from. Explore, evolve and feel the excitement.

Revitalise your mind and soul by spending some more time outdoors, in nature. There is so much to do and see, all that is necessary is the action to achieve your heart's desires. You have all that you need to get you there, for you to enjoy every little step of your incredible life journey, your life art, that is lit up by your gifted light.

The Light Within You

It's all about achieving the little things and then the big things will follow. Your fulfilled self and manifestations will appear right in front of your eyes. – GS

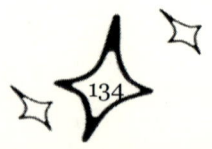

The Power of Gratitude

The power of gratitude – understand how being thankful for what you already have and visualising in silence can ground you and open up your mind to new possibilities.

Being thankful will create happiness

When you send out the right signals to the universe and are able to show that you are grateful, more of what you are grateful for will be attracted back to you. The more that you are able to show gratitude and thanks for the things you truly love and appreciate, the more of it you will receive in the future. It even applies to the small things in life, as well as the big.

For example, when you are shopping in your local supermarket and you are paying for your goods, take the opportunity to be grateful for every single aspect of the experience. Whilst you are in a queue at the till, mentally make a list of everything there that you can be grateful for and channel into the gratitude. It could be the money that you have to pay for the food, it could be the goods themselves, it could be the fact that you have the ability to move around the store or it could be that you live somewhere safe and are therefore able to visit the store. Try to think of as many things as you possibly can. Then, once you get to the till, instead of just taking your bags and leaving, choose to wish the member of staff a good day. Witness the light that shines in that person's face as you bless them and wish them well. With this one simple gesture, you are making another individual feel good and that is powerful. You will probably find that when you say those kind words to others, you feel a sense of gratification yourself, a sense of enlightenment. Even when you are sharing your manners with people, the simplest of things, you are role-modelling a grateful, well-respectable person who doesn't take things for granted. You are stopping and showing the light that's inside of you, instead of choosing the ungrateful road of darkness. Focusing on being grateful is important in many areas of life but it is also important because you never know when your time is up. Being grateful for those people around you that you love and adore needs to be a daily priority. You never know when you might need those people you love the most, so make sure they know how much you love and appreciate them. In doing so, you are also serving them with your loving, beautiful gift. You are sharing your light; you are sharing your unconditional love and you are showing them that they matter. Be grateful to the Higher Power for providing you with what you have in your life, right here, right now, the good, the bad and the ugly. Everything in your life is with you for a reason and it's important to be grateful for every aspect of that process.

As I mentioned when we were talking about the law of attraction earlier, if you are ungrateful and complaining, you will likely remain in that situation and you are closing off the chances of receiving anything different. Where attention goes, energy flows and what you focus on you will attract more of.

How can you adopt an empowering *attitude of gratitude*? Try waking up every day and expressing to yourself what you are grateful for. Even if you have to lie in bed for a while and reflect on everything that you want to say thank you for, do it and take the time to do so. It will make you feel invested in gratefulness and inspired for the rest of the incredible day ahead. Every single day is a blessing worth noticing.

It can also be useful to start sharing what you are grateful for with other people. For example, if you are having a conversation with a colleague at work, instead of focusing on everything that is wrong about the workplace and people, discuss the elements that you can be thankful for. Sit back and observe how that makes you feel.

You could even start to write things down. For this, I like to use The Secret Gratitude Book by Rhonda Byrne, a book where I write on one side what I am currently grateful for and on the other side, I write down what I will be grateful for in the future. On the future side, I write it as if I already have what it is I am going to be grateful for, so that I am sending out the right signals to attract those things (similar to the vision board I explained earlier in the book). Gratitude lists are a powerful tool that can really help you to reflect inwards and dedicate time towards being grateful. It helps you to get into the habit of having an attitude of gratitude. I like to show my gratitude through prayer too, acknowledging the Higher Power for the gift of life that I possess.

Learn to show appreciation towards your life accomplishments, even though it can be very hard. But like we mentioned earlier, sometimes you just have to do. So, sit there each day and say to yourself, '*I have done really well today*'. Make a list of a few things that you have achieved that day and be proud of yourself for all the small milestones that you achieved. Doing this will enable you to consciously reflect on your efforts too, as you will be able to identify areas that you need to focus and work on for the next day, which will ultimately equate to progress.

There is no need to compare yourself to others, give yourself the credit you deserve and remember that you are on your own, unique journey. Ensure that you are aware of acknowledging those around you and that you thank those who show support, help or generally care about you. A lot of people wait a long time to be acknowledged or to acknowledge others but doing so can have wonderful effects and help in building intimate connections with people. After all, relationships are precious and maintaining them is vital to watching them grow. They require *effort*.

Be a magnet

'*If you are not in the process of becoming the person you want to be, you are automatically engaged in becoming the person you don't want to be.*' – Dale Carnegie.

The Power of Gratitude

Attracting what you want in life is important, so you need to be consciously aware of your behaviour, thoughts and actions. The attitudes and the way that you talk about situations and other people can often be a direct reflection on the way that you view yourself. The people that we associate ourselves with (friends, family, mentors and even strangers that surround us) can shape the person that we ultimately become. The idea that *'association can breed similarity in yourself'* is quite a large concept but one to be recognised.

It is important that you learn to let go of those who bring you down, those who destroy your powerful, positive energy and instead, surround yourself with those that bring out the best in you. When you see a glass that is half full, would you say that it is half full or would you say it is half empty? Try taking control over your language, as this has a direct result on the way you think about things. Spending time with inspirational people, people that really care for you and want the best for you, should inspire you to achieve your dreams and reach your fullest potential.

For example, before I became a teacher, I worked as a one-to-one for those with special educational needs (SEN) and also as a higher-level teaching assistant (HLTA). In my heart I always knew that I had a desire to teach, because I love to learn, I absolutely love children and I love to teach. By surrounding myself with professional, hard-working, positive teachers, I felt that I too could become someone like them. It gave me reassurance and it helped to set an example for me. I learned the importance of an organised work ethic and it helped me to adopt the right attitude towards learning and achieving for the industry. I have realised, looking back, that all of those tools and skills that I picked up along the way are the tools and skills that I am now utilising in my everyday practice. I have become what I focused on. Choose who you spend your time with carefully. Someone close to me once said *'if you are sat in a room with people that are more intelligent than you, you are sitting in a good room'*.

'The more that you read, the more things you will know. The more that you learn, the more places you'll go.' – Dr. Seuss.

Visualisation

Feel it, see it, believe it. Not able to see it literally? Try visualising it using your *'mind's eye'*. Aphantasia is a term used to describe the inability to process mental images in your mind and for some people, it is a matter of learning something in order to be able to see it. Personally, I have an experience of this too.

For a very long time, I understood the power of visualisation, I knew that I was a conscious, powerful creator in my own life (with the guidance and control of the Higher Power) and I knew that these would help me to design a life I loved. But it's not always easy to put our lessons into practice. For as long as I can remember, I have wanted to write a book, and yet time and time again there was something stopping me. Ultimately, I lacked focus and was unable to see what I wanted to say or what I wanted to share with others. But with time I learned that with persistence, my mind's eye and visualisation I could create my vision over time. If I had a clear vision of myself as a writer and was able to visualise myself one day living that life, I knew that the ideas would soon come to me. I realised that I had to go through several experiences to develop into the person that I am today, the person writing this book. Sometimes, we just need to be patient and not be so tough on ourselves and we have to remember that we don't always need to know the way. The most important thing is that we are prepared to listen to our longing, follow what feels like our calling and trust that we shall be guided in the right direction. We have to trust in our own voice and our own internal guidance system, because when the time is right (as long as you are preparing yourself and setting yourself up for success), all that is within you will unleash in the magical way intended. And a healthy dose of patience is key because everything happens to divine timing and when the time is right, it will all happen.

You don't need to close your eyes to visualise, you can powerfully visualise with your eyes wide open. You just need to be able to access your feelings, listen to your internal voice and trust in yourself. Don't believe for one moment that you cannot visualise in your mind because if you affirm that to yourself, you are blocking that potential. You are creating your own barriers, your own restrictions. You can break those barriers by training your inner force and by being persistent with your efforts.

Aphantasia can now be understood as the inability to see with your mind's eye, based on an untrained mental muscle. The potential still exists, you just have to open up your mind to the incredible, life-changing possibility. You wouldn't expect to be able to lift a heavy weight when you have never lifted any kind of weight before. And visualisation is much the same. Don't expect to be able to create a detailed movie style vision if you have never done it before. It all takes time and just know that the more you use it, the better it will get.

Everyone has their own unique power-sense that can be used to access different states of being. Imagination is key when it comes to creation... you can create absolutely anything. Visualisation rituals not only help to keep you focused and to step into the feelings of your goal, but they also create positive impressions on our subconscious. If we believe that we can have it and we repeatedly reinforce that in our subconscious belief systems, our minds will help us to do whatever it takes to make it happen.

'If you can see it in your mind, you can hold it in your hand.' – Bob Proctor.

Self-reflection

Reflection is key to self-development and it is an important habit to acquire if you want to continue to grow. It is quite easy to get caught up in the day-to-day aspects of life and we often forget to pause, take a step back and observe the bigger picture. When you slow down it can help you to think about your life and gain clarity, remind yourself how grateful you are and learn more about yourself. Why is it so important that we self-reflect on a steady basis?

Self-reflecting can help you to build on your emotional self-awareness. You can take time to ask

The Power of Gratitude

yourself important questions and gain an understanding of your emotions, your strengths, your weaknesses and to learn about the factors that drive you forward in a positive way. Once you can understand the things that are most important to yourself and your identity, you can then use the light inside of you to grow your potential.

Your level of integrity increases when you take time to observe your core, innate values. When you have clarity of your values, you can strengthen your decision-making and the power that you possess.

Reflecting helps us to stop for a moment and just *think*. Constantly doing and moving in the fast lane can be easily done, especially when you consider the fast-paced world that we live in today. Taking some time out to *just be* and reflect can help you to think of new ideas and grow in ways that you had never imagined.

What sort of questions might you ask yourself when you are reflecting?

> Who am I?
> What am I most proud of?
> What am I truly grateful for?
> What is important in my life?
> How am I using my time?
> Who am I spending my time with? Are these people supporting me or holding me back?
> What are my goals? Is there anything or anyone stopping me from reaching them? What do I need to do?
> Who can I go to in order to gain advice?
> How can I support my mental state and stay positively strong?

> What have I learned today, this week, this month, this year? How can I utilise this knowledge?
> Where does my energy go? Is it going in the right places?

As we have already considered, adopting an *'attitude of gratitude'* is a worthy and healthy choice that has the ability to truly transform your life. Being more grateful will make you feel happier and much more optimistic about life. Having this outlook can really improve the relationships you have with other people. Since you were a child, you were probably taught how important it is to say *'please'* and *'thank you'*. This childhood lesson is incredibly powerful and should still resonate with you even in adulthood.

Be grateful for people, their contributions, their talents and all of their actions. Learning to be open about what you are thankful for, and communicating that clearly, can enlighten you and make you feel free. One of the quickest ways to improve your mood and lift yourself up is to count your blessings and share blessings with others. It can also help your problem-solving skills as you open up your mind to new promises and connections. You enter a problem-solving situation with a view to improve rather than to sit in despair of the challenge and remain stagnate. Behind every problem lies an opportunity to learn and grow. Like I say to my children in class, *'be a problem solver not a problem maker'*!

Gratitude is truly a choice and it can become a habit that is a part of you and your lifestyle. Consciously practice being grateful for the people, situations

The Power of Gratitude

and resources around you and watch as you attract better relationships and results. The habit of being grateful will strengthen the more you make the right, healthy choices for yourself.

One of the best things you can do to impact your life significantly is to create a habit of being thankful. It will be then that you realise just how beautiful life can be for you. – GS

Words

Words – understand how you can use words to create impact, create difference and inspire not only yourself, but all those around you too.

Music and words

You may have heard people say before that music is a universal language and perhaps that is true in the sense that music creates feelings and emotions in everybody, no matter the language of the song. Some people believe that music can allow you to communicate across cultural and linguistic boundaries and that it can ultimately be used as a powerful tool to impact on other people. For me, since I was young, I have always said that two of my favourite things in this world are music and words. Being a lover of words and having a strong appreciation for the written craft, I believe that music has an exceptional combination of elements that make us *feel* in certain ways. I love it when I hear a song that conveys a meaningful message, I feel as though I can really connect with it and make links in my own mind to a previous experience. In that sense, music can often take us on a journey into our memories.

Every human culture has music, so music is a universal feature of every human experience. It is important that you celebrate music and the impact it may have on your life. Discovering what type of music touches your heart the most is significant, because you can then use music to create a purposeful effect on you to influence your intentions. For example, when I'm feeling quite emotional and driving home from work, I might decide to play Alicia Keys on my car CD player. The song '*Wait till you see me smile*' is one such song that I like to play. The song reminds me of how strong I am and how I know that *I can*, and *I will*, get over anything that is upsetting me or causing pain in my life. I remember that *it is just a moment* and that *the moment shall pass*. I remind myself how important it is to smile, and this song enables me to do that. Finding a song that truly resonates with you can have a magical impact and may even motivate you to do something you originally found difficult to start.

There are specific features of melody that contribute to the expression of emotion in music. A higher pitch, more ups and downs in pitch and rhythm, complimented with a faster tempo, often convey happiness, while the opposite can arouse sadness in the listener. Interestingly, comparisons can be drawn when you are listening to other people have a conversation in a language that you don't understand, and similar rules apply as those which apply to music.

For example, if you can hear somebody speaking Spanish and you don't understand what they're saying, you'll likely still be able to sense what moods or emotions those people are feeling. You may be able to notice the elevation in their pitch, along with their body language and facial expression. All of which will indicate to you that the person is feeling excited or very strongly about something. Understanding this exchange in foreign language is made possible because of the way we may convey emotion in our own language. Emotions transcend through culture, just as they do though music. Language can be explained through a set of meaningful symbols (we call words) and a set of rules for combining those words (the ordering of words meaning the syntax) into something much larger and meaningful. Thinking about this definition and relating it to music, makes it possible for music to be an empowering tool to transfer thoughts and emotions to others. Music has a deep-rooted power to evoke deep primal feelings at the very core existence of the shared human experience, into our evolutionary past.

The power of our words

Do you ever sit there and think carefully about what you are going to say before you say it? Do you think about the meaning behind your words and what you want others to gain from what it is that you say? Do you think that you consciously speak, or do you sometimes speak on autopilot, carelessly ordering your thoughts?

From the very beginning of time, human beings have been involved in social contexts where they have had to communicate through their words, whatever the country or language be. Our world has been communicative by its very nature. Humans in general tend to show eagerness towards speaking,

The Light Within You

learning, teaching, showing, proving, agreeing, rejecting, asking, ordering and showing their emotions, all of which encompass our communication. This means that communication, in essence, is such a vital and pivotal factor of existence and without it, humanity would not be able to learn, grow, absorb cultures and become socially developed and well-equipped.

Words are incredibly influential, because they play a huge role in our everyday lives. They make us *feel* something, they make us *think* about things and they help us to form *connections* to what is being said to us and our own memory of experiences. The infinite power of our words helps to ensure there is a continuity in the development of our culture, enabling learning and progression to occur. Our thoughts are embodied with words. Our inner light informs and guides us through the voice and messages that comes through to us. Writing can be seen as a marvellous fountain of knowledge and wisdom, a fountain that is not possible to ever run dry even though it is constantly in use.

Each and every one of us has our own world and inside our own world, we have our own way of understanding things and communicating how we feel. This is why we all use words in a different way as we each have our own innate stories to tell and share with others. The ways in which you understand others may often depend, to a great extent, on your cultural level and your power of insight. There is a unity of language and consciousness, they are interlinked, woven together beautifully. In order to be fully present and conscious, you need to take charge over your words and use them with positive intention.

Speech may convey thoughts, feelings and deep emotions, because words are material and can be sensuously perceived by others. Language, however, is specific vocabulary that is expressed through patterns but both speech and language are made up of words. Both ignite power, they ignite force and they can ignite dramatic positive change.

The meanings of words are an exchange of your thoughts. When you are speaking you are creating an image of thought in the listener's mind, you are breaking boundaries by enabling the other person to relate and understand what it is you mean. This means that words can internally manipulate and advance situations. All words have a meaning and a *chosen* word represents the thing that we are talking about.

So, use your words to convey and transform situations with intention. When I am teaching, for example, I use positive language to rid a negative situation. If I see a child doing the wrong thing in class, distracting others perhaps, I will say *'I love the way the Diamond table is focusing and concentrating so hard!'* Doing this in a subliminal way reminds those off-task to do the right thing, because deep down, they would like to receive a compliment and attention for doing something amazing.

Transform, transcend, transpire

Are you sitting there wondering about the possibility of using your words to transform, transcend through emotion and transpire into greatness? Do you want to touch hearts and potentially change lives? How do you want to make

The Light Within You

other people feel when they listen to you? How do you want to be remembered through your words and the meanings you convey? What words do you want people to relate to, connect with and feel inspired by?

I recently had a moment of realisation when I was thinking about the way that I speak. I can sometimes feel as though I am in a rush and as a direct consequence, I speak quickly, and this can occasionally have an effect on the way that people understand me. If I'm speaking fast, those who are listening have to process the information fast and so, I am not really giving them a lot of time to think about what it is I have to say or how to feel. It's like the words spoken during moments of rushing are lost, their meaning diluted, and they become not as powerful and impactful as they could have been if they were communicated in a more composed manner. That is when I decided that I wanted to speak with more intention and to slow down my pace. Since adopting this mindset, I have realised that I feel a greater level of peace. Slowing down my diction of words has allowed me to take more time to think about what it is I'm trying to say. I can collect my emotions, attach meanings to the words I speak and ensure I am using the right words to express the right emotion or feeling.

I have also spent some time thinking about the importance of being a good listener. Being a good talker is important, of course, and you can improve those skills by just slowing down and thinking about your words more carefully. But when you are talking, you are expressing your thoughts and ideas about what it is you already know. But to build up a stronger bank of ideas, knowledge and wisdom, it is essential that you value *listening* just as much as you value *talking*. When you are listening to somebody else speak, you are being introduced to their own view of the world, their own understanding of things. You may learn new perspectives and gain clarity on concepts that were once misunderstood. Striking the balance between slowing down your words and the way that you communicate is an intention that each individual has to think about. Give yourself time to process your thoughts. Give others time to process your words. When you do this, you may witness a significant result because you may feel that people just understand you better, that they can relate to you better. Your very essence of human existence becomes amplified and you become a much more powerful, more purposeful individual with clarity of thought through the delivery of your words.

Desire to inspire

Do you have a desire to inspire? Do you think about the impact that others have on you and how they make you feel in a positive state, fired up internally to achieve absolute greatness? Do you try and make a connection with the way that other people make you feel and how you could use this same strategy to make other people feel a similar way? Are you intentional or are you not bothered? Would you like to be more bothered?

Using your words wisely is important, especially if you want to move on to creating, discovering and connecting with greatness. For example, when I decided to write this book, I knew that my title had to be important. It was not okay to just find some words and put them together to showcase a particular meaning behind my book. I really had to spend some time thinking about it after spending several years collating the knowledge that I knew I would use for this book. So, the title had to be important and it had to represent the book's contents.

The words in my title were put together over an extended period of time. I had to live with those words and see if they still resonated with me after time had passed. The reason why I think doing that is so important, is because sometimes, you may be feeling in a way that is only temporary. Your vision and outlook of life may not be a real example of your genuine, solid, concreted being. I needed to be sure that the words I used could have the same effect on others as they did on me. When, even after a while, the title still helped me to feel alive and inspired on the inside, I knew that they were the right words to choose. When I am teaching English at school, I talk to the children about the importance of choosing the right descriptive device in their writing. We talk a lot about what device the author picks and then we try to understand how they want the reader to feel as a result. Learning this technique from a very young age is just as important, because children need to know just how powerful our words are and that if you can become wholeheartedly deliberate with them, you may be making a huge difference using them.

Just as using our words wisely is important, it is also wise to be *kind* with our words. How often do you wish somebody you don't know a lovely day? How often do you stop and ask somebody if they're okay, even if you don't know them? Why do you think we have been trained since we were young to always use our manners, say please and thank you at every opportunity? Why did we used to get into trouble if we forgot our manners? Doesn't this show you just how significant using our manners is for human connection and empowerment?

Genuinely meaning what you say is what matters, not just using words meaninglessly. People know the difference when you mean something and when you don't mean something. That's why a lot of people say, '*but do you mean it?*' or '*say it and mean it*' because as a human being we want to be able to feel when somebody means what they say. A lot of people can just say words meaninglessly, putting together a set of words just for the sake of it. But how many people utilise the power to inspire through their words? Who are those that are motivated and desire to shift ways of thinking, break boundaries and move others? Is this something that motivates you? Do you have a desire to inspire, through the power of your words?

As long as you strive to know truly what it is you want and what your personal life craft, internal art is, at your core, life will unfold your milestone steps that you need to take on your journey. You don't need to know how, just know and believe that you will. – GS

The Sunflower Shine

The Sunflower Shine – embrace love and joy by sharing your energy and create a sense of belonging. Be a part of something that has purpose, both internally and externally.

You are not alone

Have you ever thought about what your favourite flower is and if not, have a think now? Okay, so what is your favourite flower?

Perhaps the thought alone doesn't really mean anything to you, that's fine, but hopefully it soon will. I believe that there is such thing as a sunflower shine because to me, sunflowers are absolutely beautiful, they flourish with life and they are among the most wonderful of creations. To me, they are strong, bright, cheerful and forgiving. They can give somebody else joy and in doing so, they can make other people shine on the inside (even if it is for a short period of time). Their life bursts from their infectious yellow colour, their shine of happiness.

If you know somebody that may be suffering at the moment or are in a dark place, then reassure them that they are not by themselves, be the sunflower in their moment of darkness. This person may even be you.

Feeling down because of loneliness, further indicates the exceptional importance of communication for human beings and wellness. But alongside words and actions, you can also communicate with somebody through the giving of symbols. For example, you may choose to give somebody a sunflower complimented with kind, heart-felt words if you notice they are feeling emotionally low.

A person needs to feel something, whatever state of mind he or she may be in, joyous or sorrowful. Feeling alone and isolated is feeling in a particular way, so reminding that person that they have their own sunflower shine or their own internal glow, may empower them to rise above and stay strong.

People in grief or suffering will need comfort, sympathy or some kind of distraction, because these are two emotions that are really hard to bear alone. Sunflowers feel the same way.

Sunflowers absolutely love to be around other sunflowers. They beam and shine with life, absorbing and radiating all of the warm energy that the sun provides. If you think about it metaphorically, we are the exact same. You may find that your energy levels and positive mindset improves when you are around other people. Without realising it, you are taking in the energy from others, which is why speaking up about your emotions and your feelings is important to release negative blocks. In order for you to grow and

The Sunflower Shine

unleash the power from within, you need to be honest and open about how you feel. Remember that you have your very own '*sunflower shine*', you have your own internal light that you can use to ignite the flames in any situation. I really enjoy teaching (a life art that I possess), so when I am teaching, I am able to tap into my light and use it to enhance my performance. I remind myself just how influential I can be when I am teaching my children, so to inspire them further I use my light to open their eyes to bigger and broader possibilities. This is where tapping into a higher part of yourself can be used, in moments of intentional inspiration.

Ancient Greeks believed that sunflowers turned towards the sun because of the nymph Clytie's adoration of Apollo, the God of the Sun. Within the story, there are examples of conflict that show that you are not alone in falling down in life. Falling down is absolutely normal, what counts is how quickly you can get back up. How quickly can you restore your power and utilise your light again? The seeds inside a sunflower follow the Mathematician's Fionacci sequence whereby each number in the sequence is the sum of the two previous numbers. All things in nature tend to follow this pattern and this is commonly known in spiral shapes. You can think of it as the circle of life, the realm of humanity, the need and quest for connection. All of this can be made possible and can become much more effective if you can empower yourself to communicate clearly. If things are not going right, release it... holding those thoughts in may hold you back. You don't want that... you have your very own sunflower shine, after all.

The Light Within You

Sharing your energy

How effectively do you respond to energy? Do you find yourself feeling a certain way when you have been around someone who projects a certain energy – could be high levels of optimism or low levels of sadness?

When you think the power that sharing energy has on us, it's actually quite remarkable. As Tony Robbins says *'energy flows where attention goes'*, and so to get what it is you truly desire out of life, you must be clear on the purpose behind it. Once you have gained clarity, you are able to focus your energy on the goal and obsess on it. If you are wanting to become the next best footballer for example, then you need to ensure that you are putting your attention on becoming that. You need to surround yourself with other fantastic footballers. You need to share the energy that they have, the extraordinary talent and skill that they possess, and you need to feel into that emotional space. Doing so, may increase the speed for your manifestations.

Being open to connecting with others is absolutely crucial for you to develop like-minded, mirroring ways of existence. I have found that I share the energy of my parents and their energy and way of being exists and lives inside of me. I have adopted my mother's nurturing and over-caring ways and I have also taken on board my dad's super strong mindset. I have had an open mindset in the sense of absorbing those qualities, so that I'm able to transcend them across to others. I want to be able to utilise the knowledge and learning experiences that I have been through in order to inspire and

The Sunflower Shine

empower other people. I want people to know what I know, that sharing knowledge, energy and wisdom with others can be transformational.

Whatever situation you may be in, remember to take onboard what's useful to you, reject what you think is not so good and add your own unique mindset and touch on top. Never underestimate the power of your own touch, your own individuality, whilst also appreciating what other people can give.

Your thoughts determine your actions which make it a reality, whether your thoughts are right or are wrong, what you affirm to yourself you are confirming as a truth. Confirm the thoughts that make you feel good, the actions that will determine outcomes that you desire, so that when those demonised thoughts enter your mind, block them out, tell them to go away and invite a shift in mindset. Say to yourself *'no, I will not allow you to overtake me because I am better, and I deserve to be and have what it is I truly desire deep within me.'* Block out the external energies that don't resonate with you and learn to focus on what makes you feel amazing. When the external energy cannot provide that, feed your mind with the right content that will shift your mindset. You have to make a conscious effort to be responsible for your own mental input.

Always remember that what you put in is what you get out. If you feel on top of the world one day, don't think for one moment that the positivity gained will suffice. Personal development is a continuous journey and you are the only person that can take control and feed your mind with the

guidance and inspiration that you deserve to be enlightened with, every single day of your life.

Thinking about the beautiful days that we all celebrate and share, sunflowers turn according to the position of the sun, they *chase the light*. When it isn't so sunny however, the sunflowers share their energy with other sunflowers. They turn to each other to share their energy. If you think about yourself, you want this light and probably seek it in different ways through your everyday life. There will always be those days when it isn't so sunny, it is slightly rainy and drizzly and in turn, this makes you feel grey, cold and empty. If you try and learn a lesson from nature, instead of allowing the despair, pain and emptiness to take control of your emotions, remember to look within yourself and know that there is a light within you and this light can be shared with the ones you love. Use your light to self-love, to operate from a place of peace. Activate your inner light and share it with others along the way, no matter what.

Infectious joy

Do you enjoy diving into your emotions, or do you find it troublesome? Do you intend to spread happiness, spread your light with those around you? Does it make you feel good to be the best version of yourself and infect others with this same joyful state? These vibrant yellow flowers know just how powerful the source of energy from the sun is. They leverage the sun's infinite energy and use it to their advantage. If you think about you and your emotions, you can leverage the power of happiness and share that mindset.

The Sunflower Shine

When I am feeling happy, I like to make sure other people can feel that too. I make sure that I show I am happy through my smile and through my enthusiasm for life. Anybody that knows me well would say I am quite an extroverted person. I tend to get excited about the little things and I can show just how excited I am because I'm over the top with my emotions. There is nothing to be ashamed of by sharing a snippet of infectious joy. Think about the positive impact you are having on those around you. If I turn up in front of my class and share my infectious joy with my children, they are bound to feel my joy too. They will bounce off of my light and they will mirror the positive display of being in their own way. Be a sunflower for people, show empathy and support for positive results. Modelling this sense of joy and optimism allows others to see what it looks like and they are then able to absorb what's useful for themselves and display the same.

Research from the Harvard Medical School shows that *happiness* is not the result of an individual self-help journey. Happiness sparks through a collective phenomenon that spreads through social contexts and through infectious emotions. If you can learn how to share your light with others, you have the potential to lift them up and take them to extraordinary places. Your happiness can trigger a chain reaction in those around you. The closer you are to somebody who has a natural state of infectious joy, the likelihood of you catching this contagious light of energy increases.

We start to pick things up and we start to act and think in the way that they do, because we learn from each other, it is a natural instinct. However, would you like to become a person who is able to spread infectious joy, with or without others? The word infectious suggests that others are able to access it. Other people are able to catch what it is you have. Are you willing to take control of the energy that you share and share it with intention? Other people are able to harness and utilise your energy, from your inner state of joy and happiness. Isn't that beautiful? Doesn't that give you hope that you truly can serve others and make a difference in the most unprecedented ways? Can you take control of your mind and stop allowing your mind to take control of you?

The sense of belonging

Feeling wanted and loved by others can elevate you and take you to a feel-good place where you are able to recognise that others appreciate you and want you to be in their company.

How often do you think you are able to make other people feel this way? Have you ever searched for love, searched for recognition or searched for feeling wanted? When you truly discover yourself and what your *life art* is, you can then use your internal light to connect with that and amplify your life purpose. This is equal in the way that you can use your light to make others feel loved and wanted. Even belonging to a social group, no matter how big or small, can lead you to feeling happier and much more fulfilled. Psychologists have found that the more you are connected to groups of people who share similar interests as you, the happier and more satisfied you are likely to feel.

When I attended the WOW Book Camp, I experienced this sense of belonging for myself.

The Sunflower Shine

There are so many people that surround me who may not fully understand just how in tune I am with books and writing in general. However, when I was at the WOW Book Camp I realised that I was feeling different to how I normally would feel. I noticed that I felt internally connected to absolute strangers. I felt as though the strangers in the room felt the way I felt, empowered, alive and significantly hopeful to share their story. There is no such thing as strangers, there are only friends you haven't met yet (as inspired by William Butler Yeats). From that thought, I felt as though these people understood me and my passion and hence, were there to support me every step of the way. Having this feeling inside of me allowed me to access my greatest power quickly and more effectively as I was able to harness the power of belonging. I knew that I belonged there and the *strangers* around me felt in a similar way. When the conversations started to happen, it was magical to see just how quickly these so-called strangers and I would connect, it was almost instant. Their passion and enthusiasm were a mirror reflection of how I felt, because I was sharing my thirst for book-writing with people who also had their own thirst for book-writing. What happens then? It allows you to use the energy from others in your own way to make your ideas and thoughts stronger and even more empowering.

You learn from other people in a beautiful way and that is why surrounding yourself with inspirational people, people that totally make you feel alive, can have an incredible effect on your progress and ultimately, your success. You know that you are on the right path because you may feel a peculiar sense of belonging, even if you don't even know the people that are around you. Feeling like you belong can break blockades, enabling you to break through difficult times of procrastination and negative affirmed lies that once were your reality of truth.

When it comes down to your happiness, the relationships you have with the people around you really matter. The positive effect that others can have on you transcends through time even after you have left the company of inspirational figures. How often have you sat there and thought about something someone has said to you even after you have left being around them? You felt that connected to them, you felt a sense of belonging that resonated with you, enlightened you to question things and think critically. Without thinking critically, how are you supposed to hold yourself to account and grow in the most unexpected ways? Quite often you learn from your own mistakes by relating yourself to others and their experiences. When we question things, we are expanding our thoughts, we are not settling for less than knowing more and discovering more. We tend to identify ourselves with groups of people that share the same values as us, but what we may not be realising is that there is a still a wealth of personality, insight and experiences that can be exchanged in the process of meeting and connecting with others. It is possible to be a member of a particular group and feel no connection at all. What counts is that subjective sense of belonging that's crucial for happiness. Think about joining a group that you may be interested in, a group that promotes your belief systems, a group that can lift you up and take you to new heights of happiness.

You can have anything you want in this world if you want it enough. When you're truly ready for it, you will undoubtedly take the right steps towards achieving it and making your vivid dreams a transformational reality. – GS

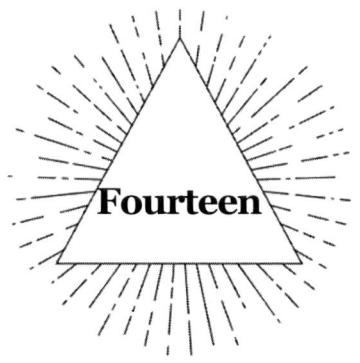

Life is Beautiful

Life is beautiful – learn how to illuminate your positive side and love the gift of you, your unique soul and being that is beautifully admirable. Intentionally sparkle and shine the light living inside of you...

Positive side

What is your positive side? Can you adopt a positive side approach to your everyday life? Would you like to, in order to be a happier, more fulfilled you? Would you like to gain a happier perspective, so that your light can inspire others? Remember that happiness is based on the 'happenings' around you; to feel true joy and a sense of inner-peace, you must ground yourself in knowing who you are as a person. What is your purpose and what is it you truly care about?

I have now been a part of the Global Goodwill Ambassadors organisation for a very long time but I first of all become recognised as somebody doing great things for humanity and was awarded with the title as a GGA. As time went on, I was nominated as the UK Chair for GGA, which was an absolute honour and is a position that I continue to hold. At GGA, we recognise people who are performing humanitarian work whilst promoting initiatives to serve the people who need them most.

It is essential to act with urgency in order to raise public awareness about some of the most pressing issues facing today's society, and I am now able to give out the same recognition to others for achieving extraordinary success. The essential point is showing goodwill towards others, offering that alternative perspective, that positive side – your inner light – upon those who need it most. You can achieve this every single day, just by shining your light into the world, having your say through being totally yourself and being proud of who you are. You are amazing, and you have amazingness to offer, so sharing that with others is an absolute obligation!

You have probably had moments where you struggle to stay positive and see things from a negative perspective, we all do. It is a lot easier to say than it is to actually train yourself to be a more positive being naturally.

The important realisation here lies in the truth of negative thinking and how it can protect us. The negative thoughts that may sometimes arise actually help us to stay attune to dangers and bad things going on around us. In human biology, we are trained to survive, and we will do all it takes to ensure we are safe. However, too much of this negative mindset can destruct and destroy our delicate soul, our ways to stay alive, influential and empowering. Too much negativity and negative thinking in general prohibits us from shining our light, from utilising our light even towards our passionate, life art (our *purpose*). A study in the Public Library of Science shows that negative thinking and self-blame can be the main reason for many negative mental health problems arising and can have a detrimental effect on our overall wellbeing. Are you happy to accept that? I'm presuming not, because why should you be?

We have established that you deserve the utmost success. You deserve to have, be and do whatever it is your heart truly desires and other people deserve to have the best version of you around them. You deserve to discover the light that does live *within you* and use it to enhance every stage of your life and eternal being. So, how can you help yourself by staying positive and remembering that you can showcase a *positive side*?

> Learn from other people's choices. If you have people around you who are making you think and feel negatively, this is having a direct negative influence on your energy and on the energy that you can share with others. If you are serious about living a more positive life, protect yourself from energy that doesn't resonate with you. Be careful about what you choose to absorb as a truth and try to notice the difference between fact and fiction. Remember that people make their own choices and you don't need to identify yourself as the same, embrace the choices around you while remembering what is right for you. Your craft of communication depends on the people you associate with. Is everything you hear entirely true and could some of what you hear simply be a truth to the other person and not to you? Recognise your

The Light Within You

own truth and don't be afraid to let go of what's not true to you.

Share your positivity and moments of infectious joy with other people because it is important to treat others with positivity in order to feel and affirm the positive mindset to yourself. Tell someone when they have done something great or be honest when you think somebody looks smart or beautiful. Be kind to all living things and watch the kindness, positivity and love come straight back to you in the most heartfelt, humane ways. Radiating total love and acceptance, accepting people for who they are and for the choices they make *will set you free.*

Be mindful of silver linings. In all pain and suffering, a silver lining can be found, whether that be a deviation that sets you on the right path or a lesson that needed to be learnt. If you search for the positives in a negative situation, you can change your perspective and in doing so, ensure you attract better experiences. When you are facing a challenge or upsetting situation, ask yourself one question, *'how can I grow from this situation?'* Questions can enable you to reframe your thoughts and place them into a positive context.

Be grateful because it will make you feel good and in doing so, it will help you to attract more to be grateful for. When you notice, appreciate and look inwards on your life, it can give you a fantastic mood boost. You may start to feel alive and proud of your situation, even if it's about something so small that you have but you feel thankful for. Think about the things that make you smile and always remember to celebrate your achievements. All of the small milestones that you achieve are something to be truly, profoundly grateful for. Be proud of you and all that you do, no matter how small and insignificant it may seem! Just as the picture on my front cover suggests, keep climbing until you get to the top, because every small step of progress amount to something great, something magical, something life changing. You deserve to live a truthful life, one that is wholeheartedly aligned with who you really are at the core of your being.

Choose a positive thought when the negativity washes over you. Think about it in a transparent way, if you are focusing on a positive thought when something negative is in front of you, is there room for the negativity to exist? In that present moment, no there's not. Choose positive thoughts by finding them from anywhere. If you can't find one from your current day, then think back to a time that made you feel good. Relive those feelings and emotions and enlighten yourself. Take the action. You have to be in control over your mind and that means you have to be in a state of consciousness, which gets easier over time, in order to dictate the outcome that you want. The more you practice being in charge and attracting positivity, the more frequent and natural it will become for you. Don't lose faith.

Keep moving, as I discussed earlier in my book, motion equates to an increased level of happiness. There is a lot of research that suggests consistent exercise does improve your mood and lower rates of depression. Move, move, move. Rebalance yourself and get back into alignment – you may have to go after and chase your positive side, but it is always possible to achieve. You have to *want* it.

Shine your light

Wherever you go, be the best you can. Show up, inspire others through your intentional, positive mindset and incredible levels of performance. I believe that the greatest gift you can give anyone is to help them find and nurture their true craft in life. Then the power of the light within you will find you, all by itself.

Dare to be great and see each day as a day to excel in whatever it is you want to do and achieve. Empowering yourself and using the light within you is an everlasting journey, it is not something that you can do for one day or for one chapter of your life. It is a *part of you* that you work on consistently, to ensure you are operating with positive energy and light.

When thinking about shining my light, I have always thought of the moon as a significant symbol of light. My grandad (who I call bandad) always tells me that you're lucky when you see the moon and you should bless yourself every time you see it. When I think about my own life, it's quite ironic as I have always had a deep appreciation for the moon. When I went travelling, I used to think regularly how cool it was that I could see the moon in a different country to someone who could also see the moon somewhere else in the world. I felt that the

moon had infinite power, it had a light that could be felt by masses of people. That to me is incredible.

The moon has an unbreakable power. Gravity is what keeps the planets in orbit around the sun and what withholds the moon in orbit around the earth. The majestic gravitational pull of the moon pulls the sea towards it, moving the oceans tides. An unaware force from the moon keeps humanity grounded, keeps us as one and united together. Whatever it is that can remind you to shine your light and utilise the power you've always had, make sure that you are conscious of it and think about how significant it is to you and your personal growth of discovery. Honestly, it is those little things, those little moments of thought, that can make a huge difference.

Gifts

Everybody loves to receive a gift, right? Have you thought about the gift that you possess, the light within you, that can be used to transform your life and the life of others? Just as life is a gift, the present is also a gift and no matter what it is you are doing at the moment, if you are working towards your gift, your life art, you are progressing. Progress equals happiness and it can start to feel addictive. When I am writing an essay for university towards my international teaching qualification, every single time that I write another 200 words or even another paragraph, I feel happier and much more fulfilled because I am making progress.

Our capacity for greatness is truly remarkable; we just need to be consciously aware of just how powerful we are and be using that power to the best of our ability. Create your own truths that can be focused upon because the more we focus on something, the more powerful it becomes. The more it becomes, the greater the effects can be. Just like our human potential... let it flourish and find what it is you *truly love*. Take a chance in doing what you love, even if it doesn't work out straight away. You have to persevere because if you can see it in your mind, you can work towards achieving it. Unconditionally loving your life purpose and using your light inside of you to make it even greater is the best gift of all that you can give to yourself and of course, to others. Dream big, think big, have big, why? Because you are worthy, as the Genie says in Aladdin, '*your wish is my command*', ask for what you want, send out the right signals and never stop believing in your personal power. Remember that you are protected and being guided by the Higher Power all of the time and this lives inside of you. *Trust* and have *faith*.

Sparkle

'*Shine bright like a diamond*' – those words have stuck in my head, of course because of the song Diamonds by Rihanna, but also because of a student that I teach. When this student moved to my class at the start of the academic year, they used those words and randomly drew a diamond on a piece of paper. I didn't ask this student to do that, they had been in my class a day and decided to do that themselves and asked the other students to sign it as a *gift* to me. It completely blew me away and then those words that were once quite abstract, solidified in meaning and meant more to me than ever before.

The more I thought about those words, the more significant they became. One reason why my parents decided to call me Gemma was because it has the word '*gem*' within it and they considered me as being their special gem, their special jewel in their lives. Be your own gem and sparkle the way you deserve to. You must be awake, you must be conscious, you must be alive. For me to be able to sparkle and be the best version of myself, I have been very thankful for particular power figures in my life who have and continue to motivate me.

For example, there are a trio of people in my life that I consider as guardian angels. Each one has been there for me throughout my life, supported me, inspired me and helped me through my darkest times. Those people reminded me to look within and find my light. Something that I have always had but often failed to notice.

I have lived through beautiful experiences and moments that I believe have saved my life. All of these times have been lessons for me to learn from, no matter how dark and upsetting they may have once been. But in the grand scheme of things, they were only just a moment and another lesson for me to learn from. In ways, I know I have been able to save people around me from their darkness and I know I have been intentional in helping people to remember that they do have a light inside of them, there is hope and there is a purpose. Sometimes we just need to be reminded and I am truly grateful for all of the experiences that I have ever gone through. I now know that everything always comes together in the end and makes sense like a jigsaw puzzle. Which people in your life can you truly appreciate and give thanks to for being there for you?

I used to blog when I was at university between 2013 and 2016 about all sorts of things that I was learning. I didn't know why at the time, but I just went with it. Now when I look back and reflect, I have realised that all of those posts I was writing happened for a reason. Those moments enabled me to learn life lessons from destructive situations, pick up key messages that would enable me to move forward positively, with power and with intention. It doesn't matter that I'm on a particular path, it's always okay to broaden your possibilities by following something that you truly want to achieve alongside anything that you want to do. Believe that you can, and you will. You will find, through reflection, that often everything has happened in your life for a particular reason. If you can't see it yet, be patient. Count your blessings because *life is a blessing*.

You may have created your own limitations but now it is about time you created your own possibilities. Faith – Act – Love. Three core truths of mine that I live by. The only limitations that exist in your life are the ones you have set yourself. It is now time to break those limitations and break the boundaries of procrastination. Time will always be on your side, harness your true infinite power to design the life that you want, the life that you desire.

We were born to make a difference. We were born to shine our rays and be another person's sunshine. We were born to sparkle. We were born to share our light. We were born to discover our life purpose. We were born to have the largest, most life-transformational impact on others. We were born to live life from a place of love, truth and serenity. We were born to matter.

Life is Beautiful

Now is the time, the only time, for you to *illuminate* your light through another person's darkness. You are *meant to shine*. The light is in each and every one of us and as we let our light shine, we unconsciously give others the permission to do the same. You are amazing, you are precious, you are the light. I truly have spread my wings and now I am flying high in the sky and the light has never been brighter. I pray that you are able to do the same. *For you were once darkness, but now you are the light in the Lord. Live as children of the light. (For the fruit of the light consists in all goodness, righteousness and truth). – Ephesians 5, 8-10*

Love, Light, Peace and Positivity. AVP, SS – Alis Volat Propriis (she flies her own wings), Super strong. Thank you to my light for showing me the way. – GS

www.thelightwithinyou.co.uk

Endorsements

Gemma's vision of hope and remaining true to oneself is enlightening for all that read her wisdom-enriched words. The Light Within You is a true gem, a book that will transcend through time and touch the hearts of the masses.

Award Winning Author & International Speaker
Vishal Morjaria

This fantastic book is an amazing, inspiring and mind-blowing sample of how it's done right. It grabs you from the first page and inspires you to keep reading. As an author myself, I can only say this... 'I Love It'. People... make sure to get your own copy as soon as possible. Gemma, you are amazing and a true inspiration.

Professor, TEDx Speaker & Worlds #1 Success Coach
Dr. Alexander Evengroen

Gemma's words are empowering and enlightening. She teaches with words and leads by example. In her book she says - be mindful, be grateful, keep moving...we all can easily relate with her thoughts as we go through these at some point of time in our life! As a Goodwill Ambassador she exceeds in her reach of her Humanitarian effort and allows many to be helped and healed!

Professor & International TEDx Speaker, Award Winning Women Empowerment Coach
Dr Ruby Bakshi Khurdi

Gemma has enlightened me to dig deeper into my own ideas of empowerment. Her words are exceptionally inspirational and have added value to my desire to impact others. Gemma challenged me to focus on that powerful light that exists within me. She displays this skillset and will show you how in her book 'The Light Within You.'

Transitional Coach & Award-Winning Author
Andrew CM Miller

Endorsements

Gemma is a positive and happy beacon of light and hope in our world. Her words will connect with your soul deeply and inspire and motivate you too to step up and live your life to the fullest whilst helping others discover their light too. Open the book and gift it to yourself and feel the transformation that occurs. And as soon as it does, pass on the gift to someone else, so they too can experience the positive transformation and become the beacon of light for themselves and others.

International Personal Development & Mindset Transformation Consultant, Trainer, Speaker
Nadia Leona Yunis, LLM

Gemma's insight and knowledge will open up more doors for others to discover their inner passion. She has the ability to lift others up with a contagious spirit of goodwill that shines brightly in all she does. Readers will gain the power of positivity and also learn how living a life of gratitude warms your heart and how self-appreciation and care will help you reach your full potential.

President & COO, Global Goodwill Ambassadors
Lisa A. Jones

As someone living & breathing the Law of Attraction, Gemma's writing instantly resonates with me: Thoughts turn into Words which then turn into Actions - meaning everyone CAN influence outcomes, by starting with positive thoughts. Gemma is a beautiful soul, delightfully sharing her inspiring wisdom with the World: Let Gemma's positivity shine brightly into yours.

Author, GGA & Campaigner for a Better World
Rev. Markus

It is not just Gemma's words here, but her heart and deep understanding that speaks through every sentence to the heart of the reader. Gemma's insight into some fundamental truths about life and the deep potential available to us all will open up doors to a future happiness we can, for now, only dream of.

Consultant and Life Coach
Roy Maunder

It is exceptionally valuable for oneself and the world to find the light within you. Compassion and unconditional love bring understanding of one's inner truth, freedom, empowerment and an authentic life. Gemma's insight and knowledge will open up a journey enabling you to reach your highest potential.

Narrative Healing and Transformational Artist
Helen Layfield MA

Gemma's light within sparkles with inspiration. She has a gift she wishes to share with all who dare to listen. Gemma has formed a habit of a positive mindset, and not only does she think great inspired positive thoughts, she then ACTS on those thoughts. Thus "The Light Within You" her book of inspirational truths. Gemma turns her dreams into reality with the power of thought and wishes lovingly the same for you.

Researcher, Writer, Poet, Spiritual Teacher, Motivational Speaker, TV Presenter, Author of "The Gift if only you knew"
Simone Segal

Gemma's words are empowering and enlightening in a world where there is a lot of turmoil and people are searching for peace and purpose. Furthermore, this book will encourage people to reflect and realise that despite the barriers and failures they have encountered, they have a light inside them that can enable them to persevere until they succeed.

Consultant and Chair, British Science Association
Gisela Abbam FRSA

Gemma's insight and knowledge will open up more doors as you open the pages of this precious book 'The Light Within You'. Her book takes you through a positive transformational journey that will help you take your life to the next level.

Author of Your Thought Is Your Wealth, (7 Keys to Unlock Your Hidden Treasures) Diagnostic Radiographer & International Speaker
Jonas C. Okonkwo BSc (Hons)

The Light Within You" is not just a soul journey and soul awakening which has not only helped me to realise the existence of the inner universe but has also helped me to sync my mind, body and soul. Gemma's book has opened the door to a new horizon of knowledge and learning, on how to smile and create smiles. It is a must read for everyone who are looking forward to step ahead in the journey of enlightenment and know the positive energy we hold.

World of Wisdom, Spirituality, Healing and Meditation
Spiritual Veda

About the Author

Gemma Leigh Smith has an extraordinary passion for writing and words. Her life has been dedicated to lighting up the lives of others with her empathetic and caring nature known to have a positive effect on those around her.

The author currently lives in the UK and works as a teacher alongside being a writer. She works extensively to give the children she teaches the best education possible, while inspiring them to shine their light and become the best that they can be.

Gemma transformed her life by turning the challenging experiences she had endured into positive life lessons that she could teach others. She believes that there is a positive lesson to be learnt in every situation, no matter how bad or difficult it may seem. From a very young age, Gemma had a burning desire to travel and see the world and in doing so, this has shaped her to become the woman she is today.

Her powerful voice and intention to inspire and lift others is truly infectious and can benefit masses of individuals and groups in society, all over the world. Gemma believes that your purpose is to touch lives through your centred craft. You have a duty to live a happy life. Gemma refers to the Higher Power frequently and believes that it is important that this can be interpreted by the reader in their own way, as God or whatever it may mean to the individual.

This book is a roadmap for those striving to navigate their way through transitional stages of life, supporting people to find their purpose, and harness it with their inner light, encouraging people to reach their fullest potential. This book is also for those who are on a quest for that glimmer of hope during life's unexpected challenges.

www.thelightwithinyou.co.uk

Gratitude

God, I thank you for giving me the strength and inspiration to write The Light Within You. It has been a journey of deep and personal expression that I treasure so much. Ever since I was a little girl I have wanted to write a book and now I can say that my dream has turned into a magical reality. This book is a true *gift*.

I'm forever grateful to have such an incredible family who I love unconditionally and who have supported me 100% along the way. My mum Magi, you have been my absolute rock... I love you and I'm so thankful to call you my Mumma bear. I thank my dad Marc for being an empowering believer in me and my efforts, never doubting what I'm capable of achieving. I thank my beautiful sister Layla – my Shub – for our unbreakable bond. I thank Milly and Max for filling my heart with everlasting love and inspiring me to love those around me the way that you both have loved me. I thank you all for being my Super strong foundation.

I thank my nan and bandad – Helen and Pat – for being unconditionally supportive, your love touches my heart every single day. I love you both for eternity. My aunty Eileen, I thank you for being a bright light in my life – you have shown me the definition of hope; you are a true miracle and an inspiration. I thank my nanny Jan and Simon – you are both so special to me and have always stood by me and believed in whatever it is that I have embarked on achieving. I thank the rest of my family in my life for your consistent support, you know who you all are. I love you all very much. You are diamonds that shine bright in my heart and continue to give me the strength to be who I am.

I am forever thankful for my supportive partner, Louis, who has been there along my journey every step of the way. I thank you for being the person to encourage me to do this... from the very first moment of motivating me to pursue my dreams at WOW Book Camp. Without your encouragement and support, I probably would have never started. Thank you for believing in me. I thank your family too for unconditional love and belief. I thank my treasured circle of friends who I keep close to my heart and for everybody that have been there to shine hope from the very beginning.

I would like to thank Kaiesha Page for her contribution towards the editing and formatting of this book. You did a wonderful job and helped to bring my book to life.

I acknowledge the souls that are no longer here such as Martin Luther King, Nelson Mandela, Steve Jobs, Mother Theresa, Mahatma Gandhi, for having such a positive impact on humankind. I acknowledge all of those people that are close to me that have passed over to the other side.

I acknowledge inspirational figures that have shown me the light and given me their wisdom in different ways, particularly J.K. Rowling, Joyce Meyer, Brendon Buchard, Tony Robbins, Tom Bilyeu and Vishal Morjaria.

Finally, I thank you, my reader, for receiving this book and using it in the most positive way that you know. Without your support and desire to read my words, all of this would not be possible. I ask that you share this with those around you and don't forget to use *Your profound discoveries* space at the back to reflect on all that you have learned and experienced while reading this book.

If you want to contact me, I'd love to hear from you.
You can find me on
Facebook @thelightwithinyoubook
LinkedIn gemmaleighsmith and
Instagram thelightwithinyouglobal

Love and Light

Gemma Smith

Note to the Reader

The information, including opinions and analyses, contained herein is based on the author's personal experiences and is not intended to provide professional advice.

The author and the publisher make no warranties, either expressed or implied, concerning the accuracy, applicability, effectiveness, reliability, or suitability of the contents. If you wish to apply or follow the advice or recommendations mentioned herein, you take full responsibility for your actions. The author and publisher of this book shall in no event be held liable for any direct, indirect, incidental, or consequential damages arising directly or indirectly from the use of any of the information contained in this book.

All content is for information only and is not warranted for content accuracy or any other implied or explicit purpose.

The Light Within You

Your profound discoveries

Your profound discoveries

The Light Within You

Your profound discoveries

Made in United States
North Haven, CT
28 October 2021

10659429R00116